Heidi Baker's new book, *Compelled by Love*, with Shara Pradhan, is a powerfully moving book that can cause you culture shock without leaving your reading room. The book is based on the Beatitudes as seen through the eyes of pastors and missionaries to the third world. The stories of miracles and poverty where there is fullness of joy are beautiful and emotionally moving. One can hear the voice of Heidi Baker coming through the pages of the book.

This is one book that has not been written from the ivory towers of academia but from the passion for revival. For those who might read the stories with doubt, however, thinking Heidi might be the stereotype of a blonde, you couldn't be further from the truth. God has chosen to reveal her to the United States as one often being inebriated on the Holy Spirit like the apostles of Acts 2 who were accused of being drunk. Heidi earned a PhD from one of England's most prestigious theological schools.

Compelled by Love is true to the Greek text and, I believe, closer to the heart of Jesus than most books on the Beatitudes. Heidi, with Shara's help, has written a most helpful book for Christians in the West. Be prepared to have a "heart examination" performed by the Holy Spirit.

—RANDY CLARK
APOSTOLIC OVERSEER

If you want to experience a gamut of emotions, read *Compelled by Love*. If you want a dose of deep conviction, read *Compelled by Love*. If you want to touch Love Himself, read *Compelled by Love*. If you want to be changed forever, read *Compelled by Love*. I did.

Far removed from stale armchair theology where the acts of the Holy Spirit are debated and eventually denied, the ministry of Jesus through Rolland and Heidi Baker has captured the current-day, apostolic heart of God. *Compelled by Love* is not just another great book; it is an epistle of love lived out by people who love the Word and whose gazes are fixed on their Bridegroom and King—Jesus. Read, weep, and let your heart be changed by these testimonies of sacrifice and His great glory!

—JAMES W. AND MICHAL ANN GOLL
ENCOUNTERS NETWORK AND COMPASSION ACTS MINISTRIES
AUTHORS OF *ANGELIC ENCOUNTERS*, *COMPASSION*,
DREAM LANGUAGE, AND MANY MORE BOOKS

I cannot think of a better person to write on the Beatitudes than my good friend Heidi Baker. Why? Because she lives it! This book can revolutionize your life, your family, your ministry, and your work as you put into practice the teachings of Jesus as expounded and illustrated by Heidi Baker's incredible life and ministry.

—CHÉ AHN
SENIOR PASTOR, HARVEST ROCK CHURCH
PASADENA, CALIFORNIA
FOUNDER AND PRESIDENT
HARVEST INTERNATIONAL MINISTRY

Compelled by

LOVE

HEIDI BAKER

with Shara Pradhan

Charisma
HOUSE
A STRANG COMPANY

Most Strang Communications/Charisma House/Christian Life/Excel Books/FrontLine/Siloam/Realms products are available at special quantity discounts for bulk purchase for sales promotions, premiums, fund-raising, and educational needs. For details, write Strang Communications Book Group, 600 Rinehart Road, Lake Mary, Florida 32746, or telephone (407) 333-0600.

Compelled by Love by Heidi Baker
Published by Charisma House
A Strang Company
600 Rinehart Road; Lake Mary, Florida 32746
www.strangdirect.com

Unless otherwise noted, all Scripture quotations are from the Holy Bible, New International Version. Copyright © 1973, 1978, 1984, International Bible Society. Used by permission.

Scripture quotations marked ASV are from the American Standard Bible.

Scripture quotations marked BBE are from *The Basic Bible, Containing the Old and New Testaments in Basic English*. Copyright © 1949, 1965 by The University Press, Cambridge. Used by permission.

Scripture quotations marked NKJV are from the New King James Version of the Bible. Copyright © 1979, 1980, 1982 by Thomas Nelson, Inc., publishers. Used by permission.

Events in this book accounted as miracles have not been medically verified.

Design Director: Bill Johnson; Cover design by Karen Grindley

Library of Congress Cataloging-in-Publication Data:

Baker, Heidi.
  Compelled by love / Heidi Baker. -- 1st ed.
      p. cm.
  Includes bibliographical references.
  ISBN 978-1-59979-351-1
  1. Beatitudes--Criticism, interpretation, etc. 2. Church work with the poor.
3. Missions--Mozambique. I. Title.

  BT382.B3625 2008
  241.5'3--dc22

                                          2008017490
First Edition

09 10 11 12 13—9 8 7 6 5 4 3
Printed in the United States of America

For *Christ's love compels us*, because we are convinced that one died for all, and therefore all died. And he died for all, that those who live should no longer live for themselves but for him who died for them and was raised again.

—2 CORINTHIANS 5:14–15,
emphasis added

This book is for You, Lord Jesus. Our lives are for You. Every breath is for You. May every word be worship unto You. Jesus, receive the glory, and call many to intimacy and love for the poor.

First I want to thank my husband, Rolland, for walking with me on this journey of love since May of 1980. I want to thank my beautiful, awesome, full-of-the-Holy-Spirit children, Elisha James and Crystalyn Joy, for sharing their mom with so many other children and for demonstrating such generous and loving spirits.

I want to thank my spiritual daughter, Shara Pradhan, for helping compile the messages and for spending countless hours poring over the material with a heart full of compassion. She is an example of the believer. Without Shara, I would not have finished this book. She is simply amazing!

I also want to honor some of the gifted people who made this book a reality. Many thanks go to Bob Ekblad, ThD, and Scott Dolff, PhD, for the incredible and considerate academic insight they offered. I am grateful to Ania Noster for helping Shara pore through messages to select the best on the Beatitudes. Thank you also to Wendy Dermott for transcribing and editing so much of the material, and to Dominique Phillips for assistance. I am grateful to Mary Chico for pulling together many of the last-minute details.

I want to acknowledge the hard work and help of Strang Communications. I greatly appreciate Barbara Dycus and Donna Hilton. Lastly, I want to thank our global Iris family—supporters, missionaries, and national workers, young and old, who live daily for Christ alone.

I am forever blessed by the example of Mother Teresa, who blazed a trail of love for all to follow, and by Pastor Surpresa Sithole, Pastor José Novella, and all our Mozambican children for teaching me the way of love.

Contents

Foreword

THE SERMON ON THE MOUNT IS INTIMIDATING Scripture and a standard of perfection I usually saw as unrealistic and unattainable. Probably like most believers, I never expected to see very much fulfillment of it in the lives of leaders and ministers, much less in my own circle of experience. In fact, it was discouraging to ask teachers I knew too many questions concerning the Sermon as I was so often told to be practical and that these teachings don't quite mean what I thought they meant. Perhaps no scriptures have been "watered down" as much as these, so grand and glorious is the picture they paint of righteousness in the power of the Holy Spirit, sustained by the unquenchable, everlasting, burning flame of the life of God Himself.

I had often been exposed to glimpses of this level of life in God in the record of the many revivals of church history around the world. Because of my missionary heritage and background growing up in Asia, I was aware of revival in China and the testimonies of the great saints who persevered under unspeakable persecution. I was especially influenced by my own grandfather, whose book *Visions Beyond the Veil* recorded God's own gracious choice to reveal Himself radically to the very "least of these" beggar children from the streets of Kunming, China, where I was born. Truly He demonstrates His grace most clearly by reaching down to the unlikely, forgotten, and noninfluential and creating in them the qualities of His own character to teach the rest of the world the riches of His kindness.

Still, in my own experience, the lofty flights of spirituality I had heard and dreamed of seemed out of reach. And even years of academic specialization in biblical studies and theology did not seem to bring me much closer to a hope of walking in the glorious liberty of life in the Spirit as Jesus described in the Gospels. In my case, I needed encouragement. I needed a real-life example of Jesus living in someone to such an extent that I would be inspired and motivated to consider living the Sermon as not only realistic but also the only viable way to approach life and ministry in the Lord.

I know that our Lord has many such monuments of His grace among His people who are often hidden in the far corners of the world, but for me that encouragement came during the late 1970s when I met Heidi in a small charismatic church in Dana Point, California. She had a privileged upbringing, living on a private beach, and lacked for nothing in education, comforts, and opportunity. But even as a small girl growing up, she pulsed and radiated with a consuming hunger for God. Radically influenced by her sixth-grade teacher who had been a missionary, Heidi's heart turned toward the poor and suffering of other cultures. That teacher turned out to be my mother, and so our families became interlinked.

When I met her, she was a pure, idealistic flower child in the Spirit, a teenager who at sixteen had already been mystically taken to heaven and commissioned by Jesus to be a missionary and a minister to Asia, England, and Africa. She never looked back, and in sheer delight, she began a life of trusting her perfect Savior as she has since preached and ministered at every possible opportunity. As I listened by the hour to her testimonies, she was to me a living fulfillment of the Sermon on the Mount, and especially the Beatitudes.

On her mission trips, she trusted Jesus for everything, always and without question expecting Him to lead and provide. She worshiped for hours at a time with her beautiful voice, most often hearing His voice when lost in His presence. She longed without measure for more of Him. Her love for people, and especially the unlovely, flowed naturally and without effort. She had her cynical critics, her times of discouragement, and her heartbreaks, but with a pure heart she has pursued her Jesus like no one I have ever known.

I realized immediately that here was a person with whom I could actually live the Sermon on the Mount as I had always dreamed, to a degree I never could have considered with anyone else. Here was someone who could take no thought for tomorrow, seek first His kingdom and His righteousness under any circumstance anywhere in the world, and in the most childlike simplicity pursue heaven on earth—in spite of all opposition and discouragement. And in harmony with the desires of my heart, Jesus put Heidi and me together. We left for the mission field two weeks after we were married, with simple instructions from Him, one-way tickets, and thirty dollars in our pockets.

Now, twenty-seven years later, we have seen a fulfillment of the Beatitudes in our lives among the poorest and most unlikely people we could find on Earth. And in these years, we found that, for the most part, we were not the teachers. Instead, all this time, God has been teaching us what we still lacked, and He has done so through the meek and humble vessels He prepared for this purpose. Finally, at this stage of her calling in Him, Heidi has gathered, preached, and written the stories of how, by His Spirit, God has incarnated the perfections and beauties of the Beatitudes among the people He has chosen for her calling—the destitute of Africa. These stories will prove the reality of His kingdom here on Earth and show the way forward for all who long for His world, His perfection, His relief, His answers, His love, His companionship, and His life. His ways are a complete contrast to this world, and all who long for another world entirely— where righteousness reigns and we partake of the divine nature—will find in Heidi's book a brilliant light illuminating *the way*.

May we, along with the poor and desperate of the world whom He has chosen, take nothing for granted but take heart, strengthen ourselves in Him, and call on Him for a dimension of heavenly life on Earth that vastly exceeds all previous expectations. Let our present sufferings produce within us an appetite for the glory that is to be revealed to us and carry us safely along the path into His heart and kingdom.

—ROLLAND BAKER

Foreword

I'VE NEVER MET ANYONE WHO HAS HAD AN EFFECT on a nation the way Rolland and Heidi Baker have on Mozambique; that effect continues and is increasing. Humility, love, and power are demonstrated at every turn in the road. For this reason, people flock to the conferences where they speak and fly halfway around the world to be with them at their missionary base. People are desperate to learn how the Bakers do missions. As a result, their influence is spreading to nation after nation as the people of God hunger for the authentic gospel they demonstrate.

A friend of mine went to Mozambique to spend a couple of weeks helping the Bakers in their ministry. When he returned home, he found himself breaking down and weeping for no apparent reason. He then realized he was crying because he "missed Jesus." His days of being with Heidi and her ministry were so overwhelmingly like the days when Jesus walked on the earth that he was forever ruined for any other lifestyle. The realization that he was no longer in that atmosphere made him weep for what he was missing. Oh, that there would be more tears of desperation for what could be.

Compelled by Love reveals "the secret" to their ongoing breakthrough. It is the gospel as Jesus taught it, as Jesus lived it. This book is profound in its simplicity, yet revelation fills every page. It is a must-read for all who desire to be relevant while demonstrating both power *and* purity.

—BILL JOHNSON
PASTOR, BETHEL CHURCH,
REDDING, CALIFORNIA
AUTHOR OF *FACE TO FACE WITH GOD*
AND *WHEN HEAVEN INVADES EARTH*

Now when he saw the crowds, he went up on a mountainside and sat down. His disciples came to him, and he began to teach them, saying:

Blessed are the poor in spirit, for theirs is the kingdom of heaven.

Blessed are those who mourn, for they will be comforted.

Blessed are the meek, for they will inherit the earth.

Blessed are those who hunger and thirst for righteousness, for they will be filled.

Blessed are the merciful, for they will be shown mercy.

Blessed are the pure in heart, for they will see God.

Blessed are the peacemakers, for they will be called sons of God.

Blessed are those who are persecuted because of righteousness, for theirs is the kingdom of heaven.

Blessed are you when people insult you, persecute you and falsely say all kinds of evil against you because of me. Rejoice and be glad, because great is your reward in heaven, for in the same way they persecuted the prophets who were before you.

—MATTHEW 5:1–12

Introduction

ONE-THIRD OF OUR LIVES IS SPENT TRAVELING around the world speaking to groups and churches and calling the bride of Christ to come in. The other two-thirds of our lives, we live in Mozambique among the poor and the needy, the hungry and the thirsty, and those who are desperate and starving for love and attention. So we have come to understand that people who live in the Western world do not have what we have in Mozambique. Believe it or not, our lives are much easier than yours.

You see, where I live, the poor know they are poor; they know they are sick and hurting; and so they come and give their lives to Jesus by the hundreds every week around the country. But in your nation, your poor do not know they are poor, and your sick do not really know they are sick unless they are dying of a disease and no one can help them. They look confident, and they appear as if they are together. But maybe they are not. So your job is a lot harder than ours.

Let me explain. I was once given a prophecy by a powerful man whom I didn't know at the time but who later became a very close friend to my husband, Rolland, and me. His name is Randy Clark. I had gone to this huge church, trying to hide in the back and be incognito. I really wasn't supposed to be there, but I wanted to hear this man preach.

He was preaching about the fire of God, the anointing

of God, and the hunger and thirst to give your life away for God, and I remember the message being so powerful that I couldn't wait for the altar call. The truth is, I'm a bit shy in the natural. So I wanted to be good and listen to the rules, not just push my way forward when the time came. But I just couldn't stand it!

I stood up from the middle of the back row I was in and immediately ran forward, screaming the whole way. I was really shocked at myself. The man who was preaching never hesitated. He laid his hands on me and said, "Do you want the nation of Mozambique? The blind will see. The crippled will walk. The deaf will hear. The dead will be raised, and the poor will hear the good news."

I screamed, "Yes!" Then I was wholly undone, totally wrecked. When I say *wrecked*, I mean being completely under the heavy, weighty glory of God. I wasn't able to walk for days. People had to carry me. I felt the power of God pulsating through me. It was truly awesome. I have never recovered from that day!

Shortly afterward, I went home to Mozambique thinking how, after this prophecy, I would carry this glorious, amazing weightiness back with me. Instead, I came back to many being frightened by the shots of AK-47s; 55 of our buildings, including all of our children's homes, were taken away; I was diagnosed with multiple sclerosis; Rolland contracted cerebral malaria; and my daughter, Crystalyn Joy, was in bed shaking with malaria herself. Along with our 320 children for whom we were providing food and shelter, we were homeless. We had to live in tents and a small house we had used as an office in Maputo. We had lost everything.

Yes! What a fabulous prophetic word. Doesn't it make

you want to get a word from God every day? Everything just broke loose. Nothing was the same.

But I knew I had a word—a promise—from God. I knew He had said that the blind would see. So I decided I would lay hands on them whenever I saw them. After all, they seem to be everywhere in Mozambique. I would actually sneak up on them and hug them as I laid my hands on them. Then I would ask them, "Can you see?" and they would say, "No, I'm still blind."

I know that may sound funny now, but at the time, I thought, "I have this prophetic word from God, and it's just not happening!"

I prayed for a lot of people, and they would give their hearts to Jesus, but they were still blind. I didn't understand what was happening. I knew the Word of God, and I believed it. When a prophetic word is spoken over your life, should you stop praying when you don't see it happening? No, of course not! You have to stay hungry and thirsty—starving like the poor who have nothing—for the things of God.

I know people who are very wealthy, but they are poor in spirit. And I know people who are very poor who aren't poor in spirit. It doesn't matter about the things you have or don't have; what matters is the attitude of your heart. The poor are not arrogant. The poor are needy—are you?

Are you needy? Are you thirsty? Are you hungry? Are you desperate for Jesus? Are you someone who feels as if you may just die unless God shows up? Or do you have a mind-set like many in the Western world—having a middle-class kind of heart? Are you someone who thinks, "Yeah, whatever. God will either do it or He won't, so it doesn't matter"?

We can't live in *whatever*. We have to see the kingdom of God break out in our cities, in our nations, in our lives.

After about a year of praying for the blind—and not getting good results—we were in one of our little mud-hut churches when a lady who was blind approached us. This little beggar lady's eyes were completely white. I was so happy to see her because I was not going to quit—I had a word from God! I was ready to see a nation transformed.

As I held this lady in my arms, I felt a tremendous compassion for her. God completely transformed her with His glory, and she fell to the ground and began to scream. As I watched her eyes, they began to turn from white to gray and then to brown. She could see! Everyone around us started yelling and screaming, "Mama Aida can see! Mama Aida can see!"

In Mozambique, my name is Mama Aida, and now they are telling me that her name is Mama Aida too. I said the word *twin* in Portuguese, because that is what we always say when we meet someone with the same name.

The next day, I went to a mud hut in Dondo. There I prayed for another lady who was in her thirties and had been blind since she was eight years old. As I was holding her and feeling God's heart of love for her, she began to scream, "You're wearing a black shirt!" She saw my shirt! She could see! So when I took her outside into the light, the other villagers heard her screams, and they began to scream, "Mama Aida can see! Mama Aida can see!"

Think about it: these two ladies were the first two people I ever prayed for who received their sight, and they both had my name.

On the third day, I went to the city of Chimoio to a building that was literally falling apart. It was an old, pink disco hall. And I was going there to preach, not to dance. When I say this place was falling apart, I mean the stage area had grass mats covering the huge holes in the floor. It would be the same as if the pulpit area in your church was broken, but instead of repairing it, you just threw an old blanket or a rug over it. It was an accident waiting to happen.

But I really didn't care about the shape of the building. We had come to love the people. Two people in the last two days had gained their sight, and I was excited about what might happen next. So with our friends and pastors there watching, I acted really churchy, and I yelled, "Bring me the blind!"

Right then a skinny little boy, dressed in his best shredded rags, walked in, and he was guiding a blind beggar lady. Even before I had preached, I saw her and yelled, "In the name of Jesus, see!" And immediately she fell to the floor.

Then I watched as her eyes turned from white to gray and then to brown. Some people may not believe what I will tell you next, but you can come to Mozambique and ask those who were there. You can guess what I'm going to say. Yes, the people started screaming, "Mama Aida can see! Mama Aida can see!"

One of my friends from Germany was there at the time, and she has a strict reality-only style about her—she does not like to play around or play games with the things of God. Her response was, "It's not possible. That can't be her name."

The answers from people who knew this beggar lady were, "Her name is Mama Aida. She has been blind since birth. Now she can see." And then the lady herself said, "Now I won't have to beg. I can go to the forest and cut wood."

All I could do was sit and weep. I was sobbing so hard that there was no way I could preach. No one would be listening anyway. Everyone was screaming and yelling about the lady who was born blind but could now see. I guess that was the message for the night.

As I knelt there, I wept and prayed, "God, what is it? What does this mean? Tell me." I thought maybe He was leading me into an anointing like Kathryn Kuhlman had. Maybe I would now be a healing evangelist.

Instead, He said to me, "You are blind."

I tried reminding God that I was actually a missionary, I've been preaching since I was sixteen years old, and I now live with the poor, but just like the three blind ladies who had my name and who were healed, God told me three times that I was blind. So in this pink, dilapidated disco hall in Chimoio, Mozambique, I put my hands on my eyes and cried, "Let me see. Let me see. Open my eyes, God. Open my eyes."

When I opened my eyes, I saw *you*—the bride of Christ in the Western world.

I saw the church eating crumbs from the Father's table when they are called to eat in the celestial realms of glory. I saw people malnourished and scavenging around instead of feasting on God's incredible heavenly food. I saw people outside who were well clothed, and I realized that they were not clothed at all.

Then I heard God say, "Many are hungry. Many are poor. Many are naked. Many are blind. Won't you love them too?" He said, "I want to feed them fresh bread from heaven. I want to put My eye salve on their eyes and allow them to see."

Wherever you are, God wants to show you the blind, the sick, the dying, the lame, and the desperate who are all around you. In the grocery store, in the mall, in the post office, and everywhere there are people who are hungry, poor, naked, and blind to the things of God, He wants to release radical acts of loving-kindness through you. He wants to give you spiritual eyes to see them in the spiritual realm.

Before these three blind ladies named Mama Aida were healed right in front of me, I could only work with the poorest of the poor. I did not understand and I could not see that people in the Western world were poor and starving too, that they were starving for the things of God. And then God opened my eyes.

Through this book, allow God to open your eyes. Believe for your miracle. Learn to live in the intimate love of God. Believe that God can take you who are well fed and well clothed and make you hungry, thirsty, desperate, and completely dependent on your Father's love so that your eyes will see those around you who are in need of fresh bread from heaven. If you are that someone in the desert who will die without a drink of water, God can pour out His Spirit so that your heart is *compelled by love.*

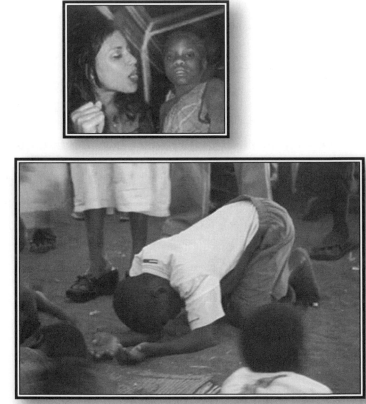

One

BLESSED ARE THE POOR IN SPIRIT

*Prayer begets faith, faith begets love,
and love begets service of the poor.*[1]
—MOTHER TERESA

WHEN GOD FIRST SENT US TO MOZAMBIQUE, people were blowing up relief vehicles after decades of war. We came into an atmosphere of floods, famines, and pain untold. We thought it was the perfect place to offer our lives, the perfect place to see God's kingdom established.

Rolland and I came to Mozambique in 1995 to see the gospel proven, to see the glory of God in the darkness. We came to heal the sick, raise the dead, and drive out demons in the power of the Holy Spirit. We came to serve God and not money. We came for relief from worry about our lives, what we will eat, drink, and wear. We came to be Jesus's hands extended among the poor. We came to see righteousness, peace, and joy. We came to some of the most grief-stricken, suffering people we could find in the world, a population that had suffered decades of war, disease, and oppression. And we came to learn—from them—about the kingdom of God.

If God was not with us in this unfamiliar world and ministry, we did not want to continue. If He could not be trusted and followed, if the Sermon on the Mount was simply impractical, if we could not do "even greater things" than Jesus did (John 14:12), then our mission work was—and is today—hopeless. We have no backup plan. We have nothing but Him.

Everywhere we travel in the West, we tell people that Jesus does things upside down. We have learned this from sitting with the poorest of the poor and letting them teach us about the kingdom of God. Jesus loves to show Himself strong to the weak first, the most unlikely, the forgotten, and the most humble of all.

In Africa we have seen Jesus do this. For the poor draw us into a life of living even lower still, leading us on the low road—the only road forward—until we become as desperate for God as the poor are for daily bread. When we send our international visitors home from Mozambique, we always pray that they take home the riches of the poor because, as Matthew 5:3 says, "Blessed are the poor in spirit, for theirs is the kingdom of heaven."

Many ask why Jesus reserves the kingdom of God for the poor in spirit. Why is it that the wealthiest people and cultures experience fewer miracles and less of the supernatural?

What does it mean to be poor in spirit? There is something about the poor that delights the heart of God. They are contrite. They know they are in need. But what is it about them that draws the kingdom of God to Earth? The answer to this lies in their dependency, hunger, need, and desperation.

Dependent on God Alone

When I was in my twenties, God stopped me and told me to sit with the poor. He hid me for years in the slums, tucked away to deal with my self-sufficiency and undo any backup plan or I-can-do-it-myself attitude. If you have that attitude, God will let you try to do it yourself for a while.

After He let me try it on my own, He brought me to the poor to learn. The poor made me rich; in so many ways they were my mentors in the things of the Spirit. We found the worst slums we could live in, where we had to climb nine floors—without an elevator—to get home. Twice the police came to our apartment to take away our daughter, Crystalyn. They thought she surely must have been sold into prostitution, as no foreigners willingly lived in these conditions! For years while we lived there in Asia, Jesus came to me every day in the faces of those poor.

Jesus is always enough. He died so we could all be adopted by His Father. I always pray a great phrase in Swahili, *Shika Baba*, which means "hold on to the Father." We can trust our Father's love for us in the middle of pain and suffering. I heard Him call me to bring the lost home to my Father's house. In those slums, I learned to do this very thing and be totally dependent on Him. I learned how to hold on to the heart of the King no matter how difficult a situation was. I learned that my Father really looks after me.

No Backup Plan

Since moving to Mozambique, we have learned to depend on God for everything. If God does not show up there, we are dead. In the Western church we decorate the altar, sing another amazing song, wave another flag, turn on the colored lights and smoke machines, and sit in a very comfortable chair. Some of these things can be wonderful expressions of creativity and ingenuity. They can, however, become backup plans. What we need most is to be totally dependent on God showing up. We need His pure presence.

In our poor Mozambican mud-hut churches, we have to have God show up—and we have to have fresh food—or no one will come. People wouldn't want to come to church for the carpets because, even if we had them, they would be full of dirt and bugs! People come to church to dance, to rejoice, to sing, to meet with God, and to be healed and delivered.

If God doesn't show up, no one else will either. If God does not heal, we will be dead. If God does not deliver, demons will torment the people to death. We have no fund-raising backup scheme if God does not take care of our children and provide for our needs. We can't and won't go on.

Each day we depend on Him for our daily bread to feed the multitudes. We rely on God. In Jesus we have all that we need. He died that there would be more than enough. We watch God multiply food to feed the masses, just as Jesus took a few fish and loaves of bread to feed the hungry. We watch God touch hearts to give to the needy. We try to stop for every single sick, hurting, or dying person we find in front of us. For months during the floods in Mozambique, we fed tens of thousands of people a day. And we see food multiply as the churches are filled with hungry and desperate people.

Once, we were having a graduation ceremony in Pemba, and we wanted to celebrate with a chicken feast. The pastors and international students were very excited and hungry, so they walked into the dining hall and ate up almost all of the chicken. When I arrived slightly late, which is not unusual, some of my children came to the car crying and said, "The foreigners gobbled up all the chicken, and we did not get anything to eat." I was a bit miffed and went into the kitchen to see what was going on. I noticed the cooks were now seriously guarding two boxes of chicken for themselves. (Sometimes the poor there are not kind; they may be selfish and hoard things, as others do in the rich world.)

I told several hundred children and widows to sit down. We were out of rice, but we had some of our fresh Mozambican bread. I had the cooks pass out the bread as I thanked Jesus for what He was about to do. I grabbed the greasy chicken piece by piece and gave it to the children and widows. As I came to the last lady, I gave her the last piece of chicken. Jesus had multiplied the food for us yet again, and the children were filled with joy. Even the cooks were amazed.

Although the poor may not have faith for the miracle, God in His mercy hears their cries and satisfies their hunger. I finally am beginning to understand God's kingdom from the children and the poor. They teach us about dependence, humility, and being emptied of all else so that God can fill us. They simply have nothing else.

We know that we have no ability within ourselves. We have no PowerPoint presentations to display. We are grateful if we sometimes have electricity! There are no glossy brochures or any slick side items. What we do have are national and foreign workers giving their lives as God's instruments. And we appreciate every gift and talent they bring.

God hears the cry of the poor even when we are not all pure in heart. He opens our ears to hear the cries of the hungry children, and He softens our hearts toward them—to help them. He honors our faith in Him and our desperation to do whatever is necessary. God's compassion meets us in our desperation.

He Is More Than Enough

Why does God break forth in Mozambique in great power? They are poor in spirit! Here we have Makua and Makonde—friends who sing and dance in each Sunday morning service—along with many other visitors from around the world. In Mark 16:15–18, Jesus set this mission statement for His church:

> Go into all the world and preach the good news to all creation. Whoever believes and is baptized will be saved, but whoever does not believe will be condemned. And these signs will accompany those who believe: In my name they will drive out demons; they will speak in new tongues; they will pick up snakes with their hands; and when they drink deadly poison, it will not hurt them at all; they will place their hands on sick people, and they will get well.

Why do we experience so little of the reality of this promise in the West?

Often we feel we have reached far and wide, and we are painfully aware of our need to go deeper still. We know our call is to spend more time being disciples of Jesus to these beautiful seeds until the trees are strong and fruit bearing.

In Mozambique we see King Jesus offer this kingdom to the poor day after day. Along with all our blessings, we also experience severe trials too numerous to tell.

We often say in our ministry that we don't have problems except for disasters. But true to this passage, God protects us from great opposition just as He promised!

Recently one lady gave a testimony in church on a Sunday morning that she had been full of demons and was told by her witch doctor to eat her family. She was severely sick and could not sleep. She even cut her arm and drank her own blood.

When she came to church, I hugged her and prayed that she would know the love of Jesus. Then one of our pastors visited her and burned all her witch doctor fetishes. Almost immediately she was freed and filled with the peace of Jesus. Her face was beaming with love, and she said, "Instead of eating my family, they have now become my friends!"

Another lady offered an even more amazing story, testifying of God's grace and power to protect us all. She had been very ill with acute asthma for ten years and was as demonized as anyone we have ever seen. Her husband was sure she was a prostitute, and he was going to divorce her. But when she came to our church in Pemba, Mozambique, she was healed of the asthma and instantly set free by prayer and a hug filled with the love of Jesus.

Her husband was amazed by her transformation, although he continued to drink and fly into crazy rages. As I translated her testimony, I asked her to repeat herself on several occasions, as I was so astonished by what she was saying. She said she was very happy when her husband died, and she hated him because of the years of physical abuse she had suffered from him. She thought it would be wonderful to not be beaten every day. Then one day he had a demonic fit and died.

After he was pronounced dead at the hospital, she decided to pray for him. In a little over an hour he was raised from the dead—and came straight to the church to ask Jesus into his heart! At the same time he was raised from the dead, he was also set free from the demons that had tormented him for years. With a huge smile on his face, he recently announced that he had not had a drink of alcohol since that day.

I remember another Sunday morning when two blind beggars came to church hoping for some kind of a gift. I spit on my fingers and prayed for the first man, along with some children. He was immediately able to see! Then the next man came forward. Two of our little girls and I had walked with him on Friday afternoon, praying for his healing. I pointed his head to the sun and asked if he could see any light. He could see nothing. His eyes were white. Without understanding why, I said, "Come back Sunday, and you will see."

Now he was standing in front of me with his blank, white eyes. Again I spit on my fingers and placed them on his eyelids. Together with some of our children, I prayed for a creative miracle. Right in front of us and everyone in church, his eyes turned brown, and he could see. We joyfully paraded the whole church to the beach for a baptism service. He joined the queue (or waiting line) and was given a glorious new life in Jesus.

Interdependence: We Need Each Other

Why does the kingdom break forth in such power among the poor here in Mozambique? It's because the poor rely on each other. They need each other. They live in a community of interdependence. They have to share with each other just to survive. Those who have much are often quick to accumulate and slow to give away. Yet those who have little are quick to share. They often give without remembering; they receive without forgetting. The poor are truly rich for the simplicity of their devotion.

I did not move to Mozambique with an action plan to save the country. My goal was not to start a revival. My vision was not to oversee thousands of churches. I came to learn to love, and I am still just at the beginning of that journey today. I am just starting to learn how to love more. I believe this is my lifetime goal. I want to love God with everything within me. I want to love my neighbor as myself.

When God sent me to the poor, it was not for what I could give, but for what I could learn and for what I could receive. God did not start by telling me to minister *to* the poor but to be ministered to *by* them. Mother Teresa said:

> Today it is very fashionable to talk about the poor. Unfortunately, it is not fashionable to talk with them.[2]

We need to start talking with them. The poor are my friends and my family. Village life is quite simple compared to Western culture. I love to camp in the mud-hut villages and enjoy the simplicity of the poor. We sing and dance into the night, worshiping our beautiful Jesus. There are no computers, videos, CD players, or electricity to distract us. It is a simplicity of devotion.

The poor have taught me that we must receive just to live.

I remember when God told me to leave the past behind and live with the poor in Mozambique. I called Rolland, who was working on his PhD thesis, and asked him if he was sitting down. He said yes. Then he asked me why. I told him that I heard God tell me to give everything away and go sit with the poor in Mozambique.

We thought it might be wise to first sell our building in Hong Kong and then use that money to build an orphanage in Mozambique.

But God had a better plan! God said to give it away.

Seventeen years earlier, we had started our ministry with a one-way ticket to Indonesia and thirty dollars. Seventeen years later I came to Mozambique, again with nothing, to sit on a street corner with no place to stay, no money, and almost no contacts. I definitely was not thinking, "Here I am to save Mozambique!" We had one old truck that we aptly named Lazarus—since we often had to raise it from the dead.

I asked God to help me understand the poor. He told me to go sit with the children. I reminded God that I had a PhD in systematic theology, and I said, "I don't do children." He told me, "You do children now."

Childlike Faith

Then Jesus called a little child to Him, set him in the midst of them, and said, "Assuredly, I say to you, unless you are converted and become as little children, you will by no means enter the kingdom of heaven. Therefore whoever humbles himself as this little child is the greatest in the kingdom of heaven."

—MATTHEW 18:2–4, NKJV

> He wants us to be more childlike, more
> humble, more grateful in prayer, to
> remember we all belong to the mystical
> body of Christ, which is praying always.[3]
>
> —MOTHER TERESA

Children have keys to the kingdom. They are more trusting than adults. Children believe in miracles until they are taught by some adult that believing in things unseen is silliness. A four-year-old child in any culture has faith in miracles. Then an adult comes along and teaches them not to believe.

I have learned so much from my mentors—the poor and the children. And I feel the love and comfort of God through my children. Recently, after flying home from a speaking trip, a four-ton, flatbed truck of singing children serenaded me as I disembarked the plane. Some of the other passengers got a little bit upset by the traffic jam as our beautiful African children flooded the airport to greet me. I could barely walk with those precious treasures hanging off my every limb.

Our children are our ministry team for our village outreaches. Through their childlike faith, miracles are on the increase. While recently in a village in the "bush" of Cabo Delgado, hundreds of people were giving their lives to Jesus. Then one of our missionaries brought a deaf boy to the children. After we all prayed, he was instantly healed.

After the boy's mother testified, five more deaf people were brought to us, including a woman who could neither hear nor speak, and she was also totally out of her mind. Together the children and I laid our hands on each one. Jesus mercifully and kindly healed them all. Not only was the woman able to hear and speak, but she was totally restored to her right mind too. Yes, the kingdom of God belongs to the children! The village surely was turned upside down by the love of God (Acts 17). Soon after, we built a church in this village.

I have a hunger for Jesus that is only satisfied as we find more children to take in, as they teach us about the nature of our Father.

Recently we have been enriched with three new treasures—children who were given to us to love and care for. As I watched our missionaries hold Lourdes—our new tiny baby—I felt God's intense pleasure. Lourdes was starving to death after her mother died. She was a gift to us from Jesus. She came with her grandmother, her tiny, bony little limbs flailing in the air. She came hungry, inno-cent, needy, and dependent. She came to teach us all—with her little dependent life—how to love. Lourdes came as our precious teacher but is now at home in the Father's house forever. We, at Iris, are so thankful for this gift that our Father allowed us to have for a short time.

At our Pemba base with these new children whom we love, hundreds of Mozambican pastors and Bible students gather in the dirt. They are raggedly clothed and often without shoes, but the sweet Holy Spirit comes in day after day and causes transformation in their lives.

The hunger, humility, and desperation of these people are irresistible to God. As I preached for the pastors' grad-uation ceremony, God's sweet Spirit came and filled our simple, open-air church. Not one pastor was standing as His Spirit filled everyone. We really do not do calm church in Africa or have typical altar calls or traditional gradua-tions. This day our happy, humble pastors were commissioned to be carriers of His glory to the darkest corners of Mozambique. They study the Word and long to see their provinces transformed. They have taught me what true riches are. The kingdom belongs to the poor in spirit.

After graduation, we also had many baby dedications and a wedding. After dinner with our co-workers and children, we took ten of our own children to our house for a sleepover. We are watching Jesus transform their little orphan spirits into full spirits of sonship. We are seeing God raise up an army of preachers and pastors out of the streets and the garbage dumps. These children are our inheritance on Earth. We love them dearly. Truly the kingdom belongs to the children!

Holy Desperation

> But in all things we commend ourselves as ministers of God: in much patience, in tribulations, in needs, in distresses, in stripes, in imprisonments, in tumults, in labors, in sleeplessness, in fastings; by purity, by knowledge, by longsuffering, by kindness, by the Holy Spirit, by sincere love, by the word of truth, by the power of God, by the armor of righteousness on the right hand and on the left, by honor and dishonor, by evil report and good report; as deceivers, and yet true; as unknown, and yet well known; as dying, and behold we live; as chastened, and yet not killed; as sorrowful, yet always rejoicing; as poor, yet making many rich; as having nothing, and yet possessing all things.
>
> —2 CORINTHIANS 6:4–10, NKJV

The poor have also taught me desperation for God through their hunger. When I think of desperation, I think of Antonio, who is a badly crippled and deformed man. My personal assistant, Shara, was driving a Land Rover full of singing children downtown in Pemba. There was Antonio, crawling in the dust and dirt of the Mozambican streets, wearing flip-flops as shoes on his hands. Shara stopped for him and carried him back to our Bible school.

Before we could build him a mud-hut house and arrange transportation for him to come to Bible class, every single day he would crawl for hours on his hands. After our Mozambican pastors prayed for him, he gave his life to Jesus. Shara carried him on her back to the ocean to baptize him. Out from the turquoise waters, Antonio rose with a bright smile beaming ear to ear. Now he brings the gospel wherever he crawls.

As Paul wrote, in having nothing, the poor possess all things because they have God. Through her writings, Mother Teresa's words help us to articulate the heart of Jesus to His people:

> Hungry for love, He looks at you.
> Thirsty for kindness, He begs from you.
> Naked for loyalty, He hopes in you.
> Sick and imprisoned for friendship, He wants from you.
> Homeless for shelter in your heart, He asks of you.
> Will you be that one to Him?[4]

We can find the face of God in the poor:

> "I tell you the truth, whatever you did for one of the least of these brothers of mine, you

> did for me."...They also will answer, "Lord,
> when did we see you hungry or thirsty or
> a stranger or needing clothes or sick or in
> prison, and did not help you?" He will reply,
> "I tell you the truth, whatever you did *not*
> do for one of the least of these, you did *not*
> do for me."
>
> —MATTHEW 25:40, 44–45,
> emphasis added

We only do what we do for Him, in Jesus, through Jesus, with Jesus, to Jesus. We make ourselves totally available to Him. What joy to give one's life for love!

Rich vs. Poor

Does poor in spirit mean financially poor? I believe Jesus meant that poor in spirit is a posturing of the heart where one is wholly given, fully yielded, completely desperate, and totally dependent on God alone. The Lord wants to cause even the rich and the middle class to be poor in spirit and know that they are in total need of Him.

God often brings me from the poorest of the poor to those who have financial means. I feel, in some simple way, that I then bring the treasures of the poor to the wealthy church, which is so in need of simplicity.

Recently God spoke to me about His desire for multiplication and how He wanted to raise up an entire army of laid-down lovers—people who are willing to lay down everything for the love and service of God—who will carry His glory to the ends of the earth. Jesus spoke to me about a mass, student-volunteer, missions movement to bring the gospel—true love poured out—to every tribe and tongue. I had a vision of ministering at Ivy League universities, so He sent me to Harvard University. This is where the first great revival in America, the Great Awakening, once touched this nation.

In the Memorial Chapel at Harvard, I was led to do an altar call for students who felt as though they were orphaned. The Father spoke to me about His heart to heal the youth of America just as He has healed our Mozambican children. Students streamed forward in the aisles. As soon as we embraced them, the Holy Spirit touched them, and they began to weep. The aisles were full of weeping university students. Some were saved. Many were physically healed. Most of all, Jesus was worshiped in the center of Harvard University!

A young student there was truly poor in spirit, though he possessed much in the eyes of the world. He came forward in our meeting and said, "I want to meet the God whom Heidi speaks of, but my mind is too strong." So we prayed for him that his heart would become bigger than his mind. I called for one of the church leaders to come over and hug him. Father God wanted to hug him. Later I saw him worshiping Jesus passionately with his hands shaking in the air. He was saying, "I feel God! I feel God! He is so strong!"

Poor in spirit is a posturing of the heart rather than an economic position. From Harvard to Mozambique, God visits those who want Him. I know God will release this army of obedient sent-out ones—from African children to Ivy League university students—who will not love their lives even unto death. I remember Jim Elliot's famous quote: "He is no fool who gives what he cannot keep to gain what he cannot lose."[5]

On this trip, I flew from the marble floors and Ivy League

wealth of Harvard University to the mud-hut poverty of one of our bases in Mozambique for another conference with the poorest of the poor. Just like at Harvard, God showed up in an extraordinary way. I was calling on the Holy Spirit to move on the people when He came like a whirlwind. People began to twirl around and fall to the ground. That night, more people than we could count were healed. No one even needed to touch them.

At the end of the last evening's meeting, I hopped in the back of our pickup truck to go home, and some of our boys ran up to ask me to pray for a new youth living in our children's center. He was blind. The presence of God came upon him, and he was healed. The youth were blessed beyond belief.

They yelled and cheered, saying, "We knew God would do it!" Those boys came, desperately poor in spirit and longing for their new brother to see, and God so lovingly opened his blind eyes.

A Call to All: Everyone Is Invited

I believe being poor in spirit is a choice—a decision—we all have to make to go lower still, fully dependent on the One who is always dependable.

God answers all of us according to our faith and hunger, and in fulfillment of His plans for you that were laid before the foundation of the world. God desires all His children to come alive with compassion and not to shrink back in unbelief. Rich or poor, if you are tired of hiding from the world's problems and want to partake of God's nature to bring life to the dead, Jesus is more than enough. We need God, and we need each other.

God calls us to be one with Him and each other. In

Pemba we have missionaries from all over the world team together with Mozambicans. Recently we heard an encouraging report: During the season of Ramadan, one of the unreached groups of people announced on the radio, "We are losing the battle to Ministério Arco-Íris [Iris Ministries]. We cannot keep up with them," they said. "They feed the poor, take in orphans, the dead are being raised, the blind see, the crippled walk, and the deaf hear. We are losing the battle."

God has sovereignly given us an outpouring of love, joy, and refreshment to the poor and suffering in Africa. But today God calls all of us—rich and poor—to rest in Him and to love Him with all our heart, mind, soul, and strength, loving our neighbors as ourselves. For this Jesus died. We are also all called to share and to remember the needs of the poor.

We all want to see the glory of the Lord cover the earth as the waters cover the sea (Hab. 2:14). I pray that Jesus will draw you deeper still. I pray that you can lie down, giving and trusting everything to Him so that He can trust you with everyone. And when you get up, there will be revival—whole nations will come to Him, falling on their faces. He changes us with one glance of His eyes so that we are not afraid to be completely abandoned in His arms.

Blessed are the poor in spirit,
for theirs is the kingdom of heaven.

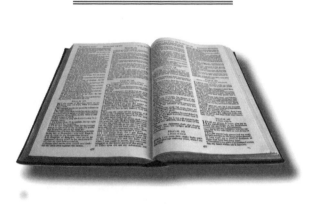

Devotional

I think that the work of the Church in this developed and rich Western Hemisphere is more difficult than in Calcutta, South Yemen, or other areas where the needs of the people are reduced to the clothes needed to ward off the cold, or a dish of rice to curb their hunger—anything that will show them that someone loves them. In the West the problems the poor have go much deeper; the problems are in the depths of their hearts.[6]

—MOTHER TERESA

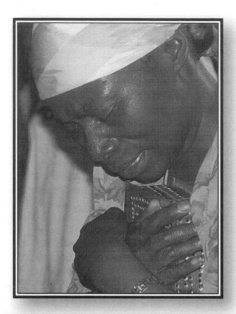

Two

Blessed Are Those Who Mourn

*Be kind and merciful. Let no one ever come to
you without coming away better and happier.
Be the living expression of God's kindness: kindness in your face, kindness in your eyes, kindness
in your smile, kindness in your warm greeting. In
the slums we are the light of God's kindness to
the poor. To children, to the poor, to all who suffer
and are lonely, give always a happy smile—give
them not only your care, but also your heart.*[1]
—Mother Teresa

THE LORD IS CALLING FOR SERVANT LOVERS WHO
will call in the outcasts, who will go into the dark
corners of the world and compel them to come home.
And they will come. Who will go and leave their life of
comfort and call in the broken? Who will go and be a
learner? Who will go among those who are mourning
and lay their life down for Jesus? The Lord wants His
house to be full. It is time for us to go to the poor, to
the broken, to the homeless, to the dying, and to the
lonely and call them in. Thousands and thousands of
"sent-out ones" need to go out to the darkest places, to
the poorest places, to the forgotten places, because the
wedding feast is about to begin. So many still must be

called. So many are mourning and need to be comforted by our Father's love.

They Will Come

Swing the sickle, for the harvest is ripe...
—JOEL 3:13

Many believers in the church are frustrated because they don't see a harvest. They're discouraged because they see so little fruit being produced; they wonder why. But they keep going to the same people.

In the parable of the great banquet in Luke 14:15–24, the rich didn't want to come. They were busy enjoying their money and possessions and made excuses. The poor can't do these things, and they are eager to come to the banquet when they are invited. God says there are no excuses, but believers keep going to the wealthy and well fed in the world, wondering why they don't respond. There are just as many lost in first world nations, yet the church is often not equipped to reach them.

Jesus awakens us to love, but the church itself must wake up! We are not yet ready to go to the banquet at the wedding feast. The Father's house is still not full. We must reach the lost, but first we must learn how. The harvest is plentiful, but the laborers who carry His heart are few. Our lives must be living incarnations of the love of Christ Jesus if we will ever have an effective ministry.

What is our motivation for ministry? The Lord is looking for servant lovers—people who are passionate and filled with love for Him, people who desire and are longing for the Bridegroom's return, people who can already taste the feast and know it's about to begin. These people can no longer stand to stay in their comfort zones. They will literally run out and call in the poor, the crippled, the blind, and the lame. And if we will go out and call them—showing them the love of God—they will come.

Comforting Those Who Mourn

I'm a prisoner of love. I have given my life for love. It is joy unspeakable and full of glory. It's in every part of our journey here on Earth. When babies die in our arms, there is a mourning deep within our spirits, but we know that the babies go straight from our arms into the arms of Jesus. Our hearts are comforted with this inexplicable joy. He just keeps on loving them in heaven, even more than we could here on Earth. In that is where we find our comfort.

In one week's time, eight of our precious little ones died. I found myself in a state of being exhausted. I didn't understand. I loved them so much. I couldn't help but wonder why. They just seemed to die one after another. The only thing I could do was ask Jesus, "What do I do? What do we do?"

Jesus replied, "Either way, you win because you loved them to life." I got a picture of His arms opening wide to receive those babies. My incredible mourning found a place of comfort in knowing that we had rescued these children from places of despair and loneliness. We knew that we had shown them God's love.

Many, many questions began to arise: How do we become the hands and feet of Jesus to dying humanity? How do we bring comfort? How do we become the love of Jesus in a culture that is crying? How do we become the kindness—the mercy—of Jesus in a culture that is mourning? And, more specifically, how do *you* become a blessing for the poor? It must be incarnational love!

Every culture has a common denominator of misery and pain. From Korea to Mozambique, and then to Brazil and America, every society has a felt need that we must identify and offer to meet in order to comfort them. A minister's job is not simply to preach on a platform, standing up in front of a crowd of people while a big film crew records the service. This is not our primary purpose. Our job is to love each person, one at a time, to stop and lend help every day for each of the suffering and the sick.

Some say, "Can we love without money?" The answer is yes. And the simplest way to demonstrate love is to hold someone in your arms, to look them in the eyes, and to offer them a smile. How do you become good news to both the poor and the rich? How do you become love manifested in physical form and see this gospel fulfilled? If you are called as a missionary—a "sent-out one"—then you are called to comfort those who mourn. You are called to love the broken until they understand God's love—a love that never dies—through you.

Yes, God wants you to do signs and wonders. But the love of God manifested through you is what people really need. So you must first see His face. You must become so close to His very heartbeat that you can feel what others feel. I want to live as if I am hidden in His very heart, where His thoughts become my thoughts and His ways become my ways. This is how we will reach the world.

Constancia

Some of you already know you are called to be a missionary. Others of you may still want to know your callings. Let this be your call: Comfort a sad woman. Comfort a mourning child. Comfort a dying man. Comfort.

Most of my heroes are from third world nations. I remember the day when a four- or five-year-old child who had been badly raped was left abandoned on the stairs of our bakery. I was not doing some crusade or apostolic, history-making thing. I simply looked down on this emaciated child and thought, "God, this is what I am created for. I am created to stop for this one." This is where I was to give comfort.

All sweet Constancia did was cry. She was unable to speak, so all she could do was weep. I wondered, "What does it look like to be Jesus to this person, to a people group, or to this nation?"

Matthew 5:4 says, "Blessed are those who mourn, for they will be comforted."

I gave comfort. I took Constancia in as if she were my own. This little girl was the epitome of mourning. I had never seen such sadness and tragedy in just one little fragile vessel.

Now Constancia has taught me how much blessedness comes from comforting those who mourn. Blessedness—happiness, pleasure, contentment, or good fortune—does come from those who are mourning. But every time I looked at this little girl, it still felt as if my heart broke. I watched her, and all she did was cry.

So, how does one comfort those who mourn? I just held her in my arms and rocked her back and forth.

During that time, our staff was small in numbers. We had only two aunties and a volunteer from the United Kingdom. But I would spend my days holding the crying children. One child after another I would hold, rock, and wipe away their tears.

Here was this beautiful, abandoned child who had seen such pain that she could not talk. Constancia had experienced too much agony to talk. Silent tears just continually streamed down her face. She didn't know about revival, and I had no clue what revival even looked like. I did not yet realize that the Sermon on the Mount is God's formula for revival. The Beatitudes are His recipe for His kingdom to come and His will to be done on the earth as it is in heaven.

What should comfort look like to Constancia and others like her? I asked God, "Why is there such suffering in the world? Why is there so much pain and agony? And what does comfort mean?"

But I did not hear any answer back. Instead, I just held this little girl through her silent tears. But God did answer my prayers, and He sent Constancia a special friend named Beatrice.

Beatrice

Beatrice was found dying under a tree when she was around eight or nine years old. She had bright red eyes, a bloated belly, scabies, and lice. She was an abused little girl. And all she could do was weep.

We took Beatrice to the hospital. When the doctors spoke to our team, they told us, "This little girl is going to die." I remember looking at her face. I remember seeing her eyes through the many flies that were stuck around and inside them. Her face was totally deformed from the scabies, and she had open sores.

I remember looking into her eyes and staring. I remember she looked back at me—and I saw Jesus!

I held Beatrice in my arms, and I loved her. Jesus looked back at me through that little girl. He said, "Whatever you do for this little one, you do for Me." Some of you may think ministry is a grand adventure. Ministry, however, is simply about loving the person in front of you. It's about stopping for the one and being the very fragrance of Jesus to a lost and dying world.

This is why I do what I do. I am just a baby beginner. God always tells me, "Heidi, your job is to love. Whatsoever you do for the least of these, you do for Me."

When I held Beatrice, I caught scabies and lice. But it didn't matter. My only goal is to love more.

Ministry is simply you loving like Jesus. It is the Beatitudes manifest through your life. Missions are when you have the love of God so that He can demonstrate His very life and nature through you. Missions are intended to be the Sermon on the Mount played out on Earth.

When my daughter Crystalyn first saw Beatrice, she ran to me. Christy saw Jesus in her eyes too and said, "Mommy, Beatrice is so beautiful. I want to give her my very best dress." (And Christy only had three dresses!) But my children are rich because they know what it means to share. They know what it is to love.

If you can find someone who is sick, help bring them healing. If you find someone who is hungry, feed them. If you find someone who is thirsty, give them water to drink. If you find someone naked, clothe them. If you can find someone who is broken, weak, or weary, love them to wholeness. And if you find someone who is mourning, give them comfort.

When the doctors told us that Beatrice was going to die, I spoke to them and simply said, "Beatrice will live and not die." You see, I know my Jesus. I believe the Book! And with great delight I watched Beatrice get well. She never wanted to take off the dress that Christy had given her. She couldn't believe it belonged to her. She wore it until one day it shredded in my hand.

Through this little girl, Beatrice, God taught me about the Beatitudes. Beatrice had love. She was my teacher for love. Beatrice personified a comforter to someone who was deeply suffering and mourning. Because Beatrice understood suffering, she was also able to understand our beautiful, tiny, mute girl, Constancia.

It was not complicated. I saw Beatrice stop for Constancia. After she had only been out of the hospital for a few weeks, I remember watching the first time as Beatrice picked up Constancia. I watched day after day as she simply loved on that tiny girl.

She does not have a poster, a book, an itinerant circle, or a speaking schedule. But she has a ministry that brings the very heart of God to the heart of man on Earth. She traded her sorrow for His joy. She exchanged her ashes for His beauty. She learned to love.

Dying to This World; Living for Another

The day Beatrice and Constancia were to be baptized, we didn't have any clean, clear water. In the heat of the Mozambican day, we had only a dirty laundry tank of green water. As people stepped into it one by one, it got dirtier because no one had clean water to bathe in. In spite of these circumstances, the queue to be baptized was hundreds long.

Suddenly I saw Constancia. I looked down at her and began questioning theologically, "Am I allowed to baptize this little girl? She can't talk. She can't speak."

I spoke to her, and I asked in her language, "Do you know what it means to die?" I said, "That's what baptism is. You have to die in this water and come up as a new creation. Your old life is going to die under water, and you will come up a new creation."

I saw her then, as usual, with tears streaming down her face. Using no words, she just nodded yes to me. She had no parents. She had no birth certificate. No one knew her age. And since being beaten and abused so many times, she still would not talk. I took this one little child into my arms, and in the name of the Father, His Son Jesus, and the Holy Spirit, I put her tiny, frail body under that dirty green water. She came up beaming!

It was one of the greatest days of my life. Then Constancia turned to me and spoke the very first words I ever heard her say: "Mama Aida, I want to lead the children's choir."

To me, that is ministry. I have watched countless times as the blind gain their sight. I am a witness nearly every week of my life as the deaf are able to hear. I have seen people whose limbs were once crippled walk again in complete wholeness. I see thousands run to my Jesus. But one of my greatest joys was to hear Constancia speak for the first time! The simplicity of love healing a broken heart is what causes me to keep going.

Often we want the kingdom to look like the multitudes to make our church grow and make us look good. But the kingdom really looks like one smiling child at a time until nations are full of people who are passionate lovers of God. I look at Beatrice loving Constancia back to life, and I think that is someone being raised from the dead! That's a resurrection.

I recently talked to Constancia, who is now a mother herself. When her baby was a month old, she had trouble being able to nurse. Together with her adopted family, we prayed, and by the end of our prayer, the baby was nursing. Her new family comforted her. Constancia's tears of pain became tears of joy.

Just after that, I flew back to Maputo to conduct a wedding for one of our Mozambican sons who has been with us for fourteen years. Constancia was there too. We embraced. And for the longest time, we just held each other and wept. When we live in Him, God comforts us.

Pain: The Common Denominator

We must acknowledge that all suffering is valid pain. The suffering in rich nations is loneliness. The suffering in rich nations is internal psychological pain. It is extremely relevant; it is deep. People feel it, and it is just as real as a bloated belly, people starving, or disease and death.

If we are to be Jesus's hands and feet, we need to care about the needs of others—internally and externally. The currency of love in the West is not always money, but it is always time and compassion. To heal an orphan in Mozambique takes a lot of love, a home, compassion, and a bed and blankets. Of course, Coke and chicken are a blessing for a feast! To heal an orphan spirit in America takes love, compassion, a lot of time, and undivided attention toward one another. Both are valid, both are real, and both are costly.

There is major suffering all over the world. We can use our suffering to become more like Jesus, or we can let bitterness fester inside our hearts. Somehow, in God's mercy, He allows us to understand the pain of others so that we become more like Jesus in our compassion. He can even use suffering because He knows how to turn everything around for good.

Whatever you have experienced you can also sympathize with in others. If you have been thirsty, you understand thirst. If you have been lonely, you understand loneliness. In the same way, we can also use our sufferings to comfort those who are mourning. God can use even the worst things from our lives and turn them into something good, if only we let Him.

The End of the Story: The Wedding

> Blessed be the God and Father of our Lord Jesus Christ, the Father of mercies and God of all comfort, who comforts us in all our tribulation, that we may be able to comfort those who are in any trouble, with the comfort with which we ourselves are comforted by God.
>
> —2 CORINTHIANS 1:3–4, NKJV

Like Jesus's bride who is prepared in trials and tribulations, Beatrice stood proudly beaming in the center of our southern base on her wedding day. Her special celebration was a joyful occasion with all her friends, including Constancia. Though she was wearing one of the ministry's wedding dresses—with beads falling off, having been worn by others at least twenty-five times already—she was stunning. Her husband framed her small body as she held flowers in her hands and had a brilliant smile on her face. She was beaming in beauty.

Now she calls the lost to the wedding feast of the ages. She is filling the Father's house by sharing Jesus with all her friends. This is the gospel. This is a girl who knows both the blessings of mourning and comforting. She knows how to be love incarnate to those around her.

A minister is simply a sent one. You might only be sent across the street, but it does not matter. To God, whether it is to one or the masses, it is the same—it is love incarnate.

Blessed are those who mourn,
for they will be comforted.

Devotional

When a poor person dies of hunger, it has not happened because God did not take care of him or her. It has happened because neither you nor I wanted to give that person what he or she needed. We have refused to be instruments of love in the hands of God to give the poor a piece of bread, to offer them a dress with which to ward off the cold. It has happened because we did not recognize Christ when, once more, He appeared under the guise of pain, identified with a man numb from the cold, dying of hunger, when He came in a lonely human being, in a lost child in search of a home.[2]

—MOTHER TERESA

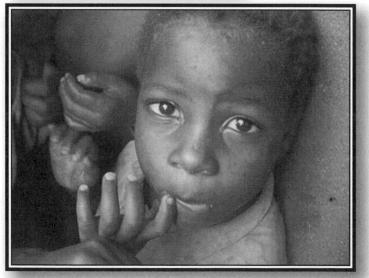

Three

BLESSED ARE THE MEEK

I don't think there is anyone who needs God's help and grace as much as I do. Sometimes I feel so helpless and weak. I think that is why God uses me. Because I cannot depend on my own strength, I rely on Him twenty-four hours a day. If the day had even more hours, then I would need His help and grace during those hours as well.[1]
—MOTHER TERESA

THE POINT IS NOT YOU—THE POINT IS HIM. THE point is not me—the point is Him. He alone is worthy of glory. Sometimes He offends our minds to reveal our hearts and make us into fools. I feel like God's little fool; He reduced me to the simplicity of love.

God once told me, "If I can get pastors and ministers to lay down, I can turn the world upside down." God was talking about laying down or giving up the desire for the "things" of this world. He is looking for servants who are so hungry that they desire Him more than their very life. They have not arrived. There is no arriving. They consider it all a loss for the surpassing greatness of knowing Christ Jesus (Phil. 3:7). God is less concerned with us being powerful and more concerned with us being willing.

Before I preach somewhere, Shara often prays a prayer

over me that asks, "Lord, make Heidi into a little paint-
brush in Your hands, and paint whatever You want in
her life laid down." We must all be pliable in the Master's
hands. For He wants to turn you upside down in order to
turn the world upside down (Acts 17:6).

God is saying, "Lay down more. Lay down." So there is
only one direction in ministry: lower still.

True Greatness: Meekness

Another one of my heroes is Pastor José from Maputo.
We copastored our Zimpeto church together for many
years. Today Pastor José is a leader over thousands of
churches. A few years back I watched him as he once lay
face down in the dirt in our church; he was sobbing. Saint
Simeon once said that tears are a sign of the Holy Spirit's
presence. I watched as this man wept puddles of tears on
that dirty concrete floor.

Finally, I asked Pastor José why he was crying. His
reply to me was, "I am very full of joy. God just told me
to give away everything I have."

I was thinking, "You don't have anything. You live
in a tin hut." And I knew that rats would come into his
house at night and chew on things—even his and his
wife's toes—but I never heard either of them complain.
At the moment that I saw him sobbing in the dirt, I knew
I could trust him. Now he serves as one of the international directors of Iris Ministries with Rolland, Papa
Surpresa, and myself.

Three days later my construction contractor told me
that Pastor José had taken every single thing he owned
and given it to the poor. This man walked in the true

authority that comes only from meekness and being trustworthy to God. He had a humble heart.

An Australian team came to help, but they knew nothing of what was going on. They just watched Pastor José sob before God and walk miles each day to work to love the poor and the children. The team told him, "We'll build you a new house." Guess what Pastor José did? He filled his new house with children who had been abandoned or orphaned and made them sons.

When you seek first the riches of heaven, God also entrusts you with those on Earth.

Soon after that team had built him the house, another person gave Pastor José a well. Now he had water for all those children whom he had adopted as his own. He was then given electricity so he could have lights. Pastor José did not know what to do with all this! If you live a life of humility, then God will trust you with much.

Pastor José later told us his mother had been praying for revival for many years. He remembers hearing her since he was a little boy as she cried out to Jesus. She told Him that all she wanted before she died was to see revival in Mozambique and for her son to be married. When we performed the marriage ceremony for José and Linda one Sunday, his mother said, "Now I can go home to be with Jesus." A week later, she did.

Papa Surpresa

I previously mentioned Papa Surpresa because he is one of our international directors for Iris Ministries. But there is much more to this man than just that position. Papa Surpresa moves in many miracles but never seems to be prideful. He is a meek, humble man who laughs easily and is filled with joy. Though he is anointed with great authority and has seen the dead raised, it is joy, humility, and meekness that crown him.

One of the first things you notice when you meet Surpresa is his teeth because he is always smiling. Rolland calls him depression challenged. He is joyful all the time. One day Surpresa was on his way to minister, and his car broke down. He walked eight hours in the rain, mile after mile, carrying a tire. He just sang the whole time, praising Jesus. As soon as he got to the village, he said, "Praise God. I am so happy to be here with you all." So what did God do? Soon after, God gave him a new vehicle. But his treasures in heaven will far exceed his earthly riches.

We were recently on a healing outreach in the bush where we had a visitor who was used to sleeping in nice hotels. Looking up at the African sky, Surpresa simply smiled at the well-known itinerant who was about to sleep outside and said, "You are used to being in the Holiday Inn. We are in the Holiday Out. You know the five-star hotels. We are in the million-star hotel!"

When you are humble, you can live in a five-star hotel or under a million stars in the bush and count it all as joy. Matthew 5:5 says, "Blessed are the meek, for they will inherit the earth." One meaning of that scripture is that you are always rich because you are abiding in the very heart of God. There is something about the humble that allows Jesus to flow out of their life. We see the fingerprint of God in their humble frame.

> Ask of me, and I will make the nations your inheritance, the ends of the earth your possession.
>
> —PSALM 2:8

What type of earth do the meek inherit? Is this passage describing material prosperity?

I believe this passage is describing the new earth. But God will also entrust the meek with inheriting different people groups as His possession. It is friends, children, and family who are our true riches. And He has given me my Mozambican family as my inheritance.

The Makua Bride

So how do we inherit the earth? In 2002, God sent us to Pemba in the Mozambican province of Cabo Delgado. Cabo Delgado is home to the Makua tribe. Missiologists reported at the time that the Makua was one of the most unreached people groups in sub-Saharan Africa.

When God told us to leave our children in the south and move up north, I wept. But we moved up north to gain our inheritance—God's Makua bride. Mercifully, God spoke to me that I could bring fifty of our southern children with us up north.

When we first moved to Pemba, there were very few missionaries living in this nearly unreached province. By the beautiful grace of God, I was immediately able to lead fifteen people to Jesus. And the people were still manifesting demons as they came to the first discipleship meeting. Each week we would load up a Land Rover of singing children, drive out into the darkness, and preach the good news of salvation in Jesus's name. And every week there were miracles.

Now there are hundreds and hundreds of churches among the Makua, and thousands have placed their faith in Jesus. God continually performs mighty deeds through the meek and humble who love Him. He will give us the ends of the earth as our inheritance.

Strategic Plan: Lower Still

People often hear about our church growth and ask, "What's your strategic plan?" I laugh. We are not smart enough for a strategic plan of our own.

God's plan for strategic church growth was for us to simply stop what we were doing, go sit with the poor, and learn how to love. Rolland and I did this, but our goal was not to start a church growth movement. We sat in the street to learn about the kingdom from the poor and from the children. Later, blind eyes started to see, deaf ears started to hear, those who had crippled limbs started to walk, and the poor local pastors in their mud huts started to raise the dead.

Now in Mozambique we have seen more than one hundred people raised from the dead! The people bring the dead in their coffins to our street preachers and our bush preachers. They bring babies who have died, and sometimes they live again in Jesus's name!

Raising the dead is a good strategic plan! The church grows when you raise the dead. Now there are thousands of churches. We want to see a church planted in every village from Africa to Jerusalem. We want the glory of God to cover the earth as the waters cover the sea (Hab. 2:14). We want to be so humble that we are irresistible to the Holy Spirit.

The River Flows to the Lowest Places

The heart of the king is in the hand of the Lord.

People will often give me expensive rings. So with great joy, I take these sparkly rings and slip them on the withered, wrinkled hands of the poor—those stricken with leprosy and disease. These poor women are finally getting married, and I slide the rings on their fingers, thinking, "This is God's upside-down kingdom."

God has told me that I could always pray for one thing: to expand our hearts to love more.

One day Jesus showed me a vision. He said, "I want to take you up the mountain to a low place because the river flows to the low places." If you are in a low place and not concerned about your position, whatever trickling presence of God is in the room, you will be low enough to receive it. First Peter 5:5 says, "God resists the proud, but gives grace to the humble" (NKJV). Luke 1:52 says, "He has brought down rulers from their thrones but has lifted up the humble." Perhaps we must be low enough to live in God's glory love.

You should want to be immersed in, and live inside, the very heart of God. From there, all fruitfulness flows. In Ezekiel 47, one of my favorite passages, the trees planted by the river bear fruit twelve months of the year. True apostolic ministry only flows from being immersed in the presence of God. This creates continuous supernatural fruitfulness.

I am not sure that I completely understand the whole "apostolic ministry" thing. However, I have heard a good friend of mine named Randy Clark speak about apostolic authority and being sent-out ones. When Randy preached, it seemed that the Holy Spirit stood me up on my head.

I like to be low, not high. I like to be hidden under the wings of the Lord, away from the gaze of man. I am not into standing on my head in front of thousands of people. I was so thankful I had on trousers.

It felt as if I was thrown from my head to my back time after time by the awesome power of God. It was as though I was bruised from head to toe. And I was completely humbled!

God spoke to me through this and said, "Apostolic is upside down." Unlike how people are often trying to exalt themselves, the apostolic is the lowest place. Apostolic is a place of laid-down love where we become possessed with the nature of the man Christ Jesus to become a servant of all.

This is God's desire for ministry: humility. In humility, Jesus became nothing. Even though He knew that He had rights to everything, He chose to stand mute before His accusers. Jesus constrained Himself to the will of the Father. He robed Himself in meekness.

Humility is considering others before you consider yourself. It is when you give way to and prefer the crippled man, the blind lady begging at your door, the arrogant preacher, or the one who cuts into the line in front of you. We are to do nothing out of selfish ambition. This does not mean that you never look out for your own interests. Rather, this means to look first toward the interests of others. You think, see, hear, and feel as you look around you. You stop, you listen, and you consider the interests of others before you consider yourself.

What was Jesus's attitude? It was the very nature of God. He did not consider equality something to be grasped. Jesus knew who He was at all times. A true son knows who he is because he has heard the voice of his father, and Jesus heard His Father as "a voice from heaven said, 'This is my Son, whom I love; with him I am well pleased'" (Matt. 3:17).

A true son knows he has access to all that his father has. In the parable of the prodigal son, the father says, "My son... you are always with me, and everything I have is yours" (Luke 15:31). It is not about proving something to someone. It is about becoming like Him in nature. Jesus freely gave Himself away for love's sake, and He invites us to do the same.

In Philippians 2, Paul exhorts us to do nothing out of selfish ambition or vain conceit. None of us should want to build our own ministries—that is the opposite of what God called us to. We are called in love and meekness to establish God's kingdom on Earth.

The Key to Truly Being Full

Selfish ambition is the mortal enemy of the heart of the church. That is why the very first beatitude is an exhortation to be poor in spirit, in complete awareness of our desperate need for Jesus. Without this revelation, little blessing will flow.

When I was in my twenties, I still had some ambition and self-reliance. I thought it was really exciting to be invited to do big meetings. I remember when Jesus stopped me. I was preaching all over Asia, seeing hundreds, sometimes thousands, of people come to Jesus night after night.

Then God said, "Stop!" But I rebuked that voice in Jesus's name, thinking it was the enemy. The third time I heard the voice, I realized it was God, and I fell on my

face. I had to ask God why He would tell me to stop when
I was leading "the multitudes" to Him. He told me, "You
don't know anything about the kingdom." I did not want
to hear that.

So, I told God that I did know about His kingdom.
After all, people were coming to Jesus. He again said
to me, "You don't know about the kingdom." Finally, I
decided to start listening. That's when He told me to sit
with the poor and learn about His kingdom.

God cannot use selfish ambition. He cannot bless vain
conceit. He wants to rip it out of us.

In humility, you consider others to be better than
yourself. You never put yourself in the high place above
others; for example, one of the first things I often do in
big conferences or outdoor meetings, if possible, is take
down the red ropes barricading me from the people. I
look at all the bodyguards and laugh, saying, "No ropes!" I
do appreciate their help, however, when I am really tired.
But most of the time, I sit in the dirt or on the floor with
everyone else.

Our pastors here in Mozambique do not have lovely
clothes or fine leather shoes. They live in mud huts. We
call them "papas" rather than "apostles" or "reverends."
But they are like the early apostles "...who have turned
the world upside down" (Acts 17:6, NKJV).

One of my favorite heroes in the faith is Mama
Tanweke. She has raised three people from the dead, and
together with Papa Tanweke, she oversees a region in
our movement. Everywhere they preach, great signs and
wonders follow. But she failed the third year of our Bible
college! At graduation, the missionaries told me that she

had failed the final exams because she could not read well enough.

Think about that: three people were raised from the dead, but she is a Bible school failure. Perhaps God does not care as much about our so-called ministry qualifications as we do! Mama Tanweke is just one of the meek ones who have inherited the earth in God's upside-down economy.

Equally Yoked in Love

> And I heard a loud voice from heaven saying, "Behold, the tabernacle of God is with men, and He will dwell with them, and they shall be His people. God himself will be with them and be their God. And God will wipe away every tear from their eyes; there shall be no more death, nor sorrow, nor crying. There shall be no more pain, for the former things have passed away."
>
> —REVELATION 21:3–4, NKJV

To inherit the earth, we must be meek. To become a bride equally yoked in love, we follow the footsteps of Jesus. We must, in love, empty ourselves and become poor in spirit to gain the riches of heaven and be filled with Him. Jesus gave all for His bride when He came to dwell among us. Now we give up our lives to be married to Him and inherit the riches of heaven.

The Christian life is all about union and communion. As Revelation 21 describes, God has chosen to make His dwelling with us, to call us His people. In Jesus, our servant King, God has united Himself with humanity. In union with Jesus, we inherit a new heaven and a new earth. When two people are truly in love, they will each give all that they have for the other. God does not want us to merely love like Jesus. His desire is to possess our very nature with *His* love.

This bride will be radiant and dazzling, altogether lovely like her Bridegroom King. She will have the same Spirit, being like-minded, doing nothing out of selfish ambition or vain conceit. She will consider others more than herself. She will be led by Philippians 2, which says, "Let nothing be done through selfish ambition or conceit, but in lowliness of mind let each esteem others better than himself. Let each of you look out not only for his own interests, but also for the interests of others" (vv. 3–4, NKJV).

This bride will give up the selfish riches of this world to inherit the earth. She will be so ruined and wrecked by love that she will run full force into the darkness. This will cause His light through her to explode into the world—all for love's sake.

We must give our life, in marriage, to another—to our Bridegroom, King Jesus. If we embrace the Sermon on the Mount, our life no longer is our own, and yet it is the most fulfilling, exciting, and joyful life imaginable. God knows how to bless us with the true riches of heaven.

Bridal Garments: Taking the Brown Robe

To come and follow Jesus, we wear the same garment He gladly wore—His brown robe of holy humility.

A few years ago, I had a heavenly visitation in which God spoke very clearly to me. I was going through a difficult time because several children in our AIDS baby house had come down with a terrible case of measles. I was crying with my co-workers, and I said, "O Jesus, come to me now. I need You now. These are our babies."

That's when I saw Jesus in a vision, and He looked at me. I was undone! When I see His face, I am ruined. But He looked at me, and I noticed that He had two robes in His hands.

In His right hand was this glorious, translucent robe, dazzling and radiant. The material looked almost alive. It was stunning: a white robe with gold, blue, and royal purple interwoven in it. It took my breath away.

I looked up at Jesus and said, "That's the most beautiful thing I've ever seen."

In Jesus's other hand, there was another robe. It was brown burlap; it had rips in it and was not clean. I have never liked brown. But when I looked at Jesus again, He said, "Heidi, choose your robe."

I started screaming, "I want the brown robe! I want the brown robe!" I immediately thought to myself, "What am I saying?" I do not know why I said it because my natural heart longed for the beautiful robe.

The Lord smiled at me with those eyes of liquid love and said, "You've chosen well. This is the robe I wore on Earth." And Jesus Himself put the robe on me.

Then He continued, "This other robe is yours too. In the kingdom, you will marry Me in this robe." If we are low, He will lift us up. If we humble ourselves, He will exalt us. If we walk as He walked, wear what He wore, and love as He loves, we too will inherit the earth.

Mother Teresa's Commissioning

Mother Teresa continually humbled herself before God and man. Throughout her life, she maintained that the most important and memorable day in her life was Tuesday, September 10, 1946. She was traveling third class by train from Calcutta to Darjeeling to attend her annual spiritual retreat at Loreto's Convent. She found herself reading Matthew 25:31, the parable of the sheep and the goats. Writings on her comments about this time state:

> I felt the holy words piercing into the inner-most recesses of my heart in a way I had never experienced before. You know the story of Saul, who was riding from Jerusalem to Damascus. On the way, a ray of light struck from heaven like lightning; it stopped him, threw him down from his horse and compelled him to listen to the words of Our Lord. I, too, was stopped by the glow of St. Matthew's holy words and was forced to listen to the voice of our Lord.[2]

Looking out the train window, she was overwhelmed at the plight of the beggars she saw along the way. From deep within, the voice continued to speak:

> My dear, you must see your beloved Jesus in each one of these miserable people. You must love that Jesus, serve that Jesus and look after that Jesus. Never forget His voice when He says, "Whenever you did it for the least of these My brothers, you did it for Me."[3]

*Blessed are the meek, for they
will inherit the earth.*

Devotional

People often ask me to pray for them to see
the face of Jesus. I pray for each one to see
the beautiful face of Jesus in the poor. All
of them are created in the image of God.
Each one is precious to Him. If we will allow
Him to open our eyes and sharpen our
vision, we will find ourselves meek before
our mighty Bridegroom King. We will find
our hearts are drawn outward to the broken
and the poor. We will call them home into a
place of security and love. We will call them
home to Jesus.

Four

BLESSED ARE THOSE WHO HUNGER AND THIRST FOR RIGHTEOUSNESS

Jesus said to them, "I tell you the truth, it is not Moses who has given you the bread from heaven, but it is my Father who gives you the true bread from heaven. For the bread of God is he who comes down from heaven and gives life to the world."...Then Jesus declared, "I am the bread of life. He who comes to me will never go hungry, and he who believes in me will never be thirsty."
—JOHN 6:32–33, 35

THE POOR ALWAYS WANT SOMETHING TO EAT; THEY are always hungry. The physical desperation among the poor often translates into spiritual hunger. Like the poor, God is calling us to hunger and thirst after Him with the same desperation. To learn about hunger, sit with the starving. To learn about thirst, sit with those who have nothing to drink.

Recently, I was preaching to our Mozambican pastors at our Bible school in Pemba. Here are hungry and thirsty men, desperate for what is real. They are longing for God. But they are the poorest pastors I know, even though they are among the richest in the spirit realm. Days after discovering who Jesus is, they come to be trained to care for a group of others in the bush.

We cannot keep up with what Jesus is doing; we are seeing our nation come to Him. They often walk in with bare feet and ragged T-shirts. When we open the school, I ask how many of the pastors have had an immediate family member die of starvation. Often many hands are raised. We recently lost a pastor whose family was starving to death. In order to feed his family, he would dive in crocodile-infested rivers for water lily bulbs. In trying to provide for his family, he was eaten alive.

We in the first, or Western, world often know very little about hunger. It is hard for some to even imagine having to do what this pastor did to feed his family. But we can learn from them. That's why I often have our Mozambican pastors come and pray for the westerners, in order to teach them about hunger. The pastors have certainly taught me.

Fresh Bread From Heaven

Years ago, while I was learning about hunger, I had a vision of Jesus surrounded by a multitude of children. He looked at me with His intense, burning eyes of love, and I was completely undone. Jesus told me to feed the children, and I began to cry out loud, "No, there are too many!"

He asked me to look into His eyes, and He said, "I died that there would always be enough." Then He reached down and broke a piece of flesh out of His right side.

His eyes were so magnificently beautiful, yet His body was bruised and broken. He handed me the piece of His flesh; I took it and stretched my hand out to the first child. It became fresh bread. I gave the bread to the children, and they all ate.

Then Jesus put a simple poor-man's cup next to His side and filled it with blood and water. He told me it was a cup of suffering and joy, and He asked me if I would drink it. I drank it and then started to give it to the children. It became drink for them too.

Again He said, "I died that there would always be enough." Since that day, I have taken in every orphan child that Jesus put in front of me, and I have asked my precious co-workers to do the same.

For the next ten years, I learned a lot about provision for the poor. With delight I have watched God place bread in our hands for the children to eat. By His grace every day there is somehow always enough food.

Since I received this vision, Iris Ministries has gone from caring for 320 children to close to 7,000 children. For months during the flooding of the Zambezi River in 2007, God provided through His people, and we were feeding about 50,000 people every day.

My heart is so full of praise and gratitude to God for how He has blessed us with all these beautiful children. I have stood in awe as God has grown us from only a few churches to more than six thousand in ten years' time. Jesus has continually given us fresh bread from heaven. We live to be in His glorious presence. He has poured out His love to us without measure. He has called us to bring the lost children home. We are called to feed the hungry.

The Greatest Banquet of All

"But when you give a banquet, invite the poor, the crippled, the lame, the blind, and you will be blessed. Although they cannot repay you, you will be repaid at the resurrection of the righteous." When one of those at the table with him heard this, he said to Jesus, "Blessed is the man who will eat at the feast in the kingdom of God." Jesus replied: "A certain man was preparing a great banquet and invited many guests. At the time of the banquet he sent his servant to tell those who had been invited, 'Come, for everything is now ready.' But they all alike began to make excuses. The first said, 'I have just bought a field, and I must go and see it. Please excuse me.' Another said, 'I have just bought five yoke of oxen, and I'm on my way to try them out. Please excuse me.' Still another said, 'I just got married, so I can't come.' The servant came back and reported this to his master. Then the owner of the house became angry and ordered his servant, 'Go out quickly into the streets and alleys of the town and bring in the poor, the crippled, the blind and the lame.' 'Sir,' the servant said, 'what you ordered has been done, but there is still room.' Then the master told his servant, 'Go out to the roads and country lanes and make them come in, so that my house will be full. I tell you, not one of those men who were invited will get a taste of my banquet.'"

—LUKE 14:13–24

Food is central to every culture and every human being. Jesus beautifully uses the parable of the wedding feast to show us how much He enjoys a good feast. We are all created to eat and live, but we are also created to enjoy. Food and drink are included in most celebrations. Without food, we die. Jesus suffered so that we could eat. He sacrificed Himself so we could enjoy who He is. We come to Him and eat His feast daily.

In Mozambique, because the people are so poor, it is very easy for them to recognize their own need for God. As the man did in this parable, we have sent out invitations all over the nation. The poor, the crippled, the blind, and the lame are running in each week by the hundreds!

Feeding the Multitudes

Many of us have been spiritually starved so long that we do not even know how to eat. The poor have taught me how to feast. One day, some good friends gave us money to buy chickens. Our children rarely eat chicken, so they really know how to celebrate during a feast. And no one would even listen to my speaking because it was chicken time.

The kids were happy, and we invited every bandit in town. Like the parable in Luke, we went to gather all the poor, the prostitutes, the drug addicts, and the alcoholics, and we were making a ruckus. The older mamas cooked the chicken one night for about seventeen hours, singing, "*Kami-manbu Xiquembu Shamatimba.*" (Thank you. God is great!)

After we finished preaching the message, the cook and a skeptical missionary believer asked me, "How many people did you invite today?" I told them, "Everyone we could find!" The Father invites us all to the great wedding feast in heaven, so on Earth, we like to do the same. We read the Book where Luke said to invite them all—the poor, the crippled, the blind, the lame—and we did!

We told them to feed the visitors first, and they got a

bit scared. They had counted 1,138 pieces of chicken—we knew that was a greasy job—but then they started thinking about all the people invited and thought, "We don't have enough." There were more than 2,200 people.

Often what we do is impossible in the natural, but we know that God can do anything! My theme and my theology is, "God is God. I am not. Hooray!"

So we all sat down to a chicken feast. Just as the passage in Luke 14 promises, all the bandits, drunkards, prostitutes, visitors, and children ate together. And there was more than enough!

There were even bags of chicken left over for the mamas to take home with them. It was a beautiful miracle confirmed by a very worried cook.

Watching those children devour greasy chicken helped to show me how to feast on Jesus. I want to partake of every part of Him. I want to hunger after Him, to delight in Him. I want to anticipate His communion with me. I want to thirst for His kingdom of righteousness to be established on the earth.

The Poor in Disguise: Feeding the West

The poor will never say no to a feast. They will come to eat spiritual food and to eat physical food. But the Lord is setting out a spiritual banquet for His Western bride too.

The challenge in the West is that many are too full. We have smorgasbords, buffets, and restaurants at almost every corner. So, people in the Western world are often just not hungry.

In my travels to the Western world, I see that the church is often surviving on spiritual crumbs. I was in a meeting, and I was on my face as usual when I had an impression of this concerning the Western church. I was looking out on a conference crowd of people who all seemed to be well fed. But superimposed over these people, I saw bloated bellies like my malnourished African children. I saw these people scavenging in the garbage like our homeless children, barely surviving off crumbs under the table. Now, we need to get them to understand how God teaches us that He can feed all the hungry, both rich and poor.

God tells us to invite those who are hungry and give to those who cannot give back. In the West, we invite the lost again and again, but, for the most part, they don't come. We wonder why they do not come to our meetings, but often it's because they are not very hungry.

Many people in the West have not yet seen Jesus for themselves. We can pray for people to become hungry for Him. We can pray that we carry the bread of His presence to the people. But when they see that we have so much fresh bread from heaven and we are willing to give it to them, no one will be able to resist, not even the well fed.

In Mozambique, it is different. No one would refuse food, so they readily and enthusiastically say yes when it's offered. But the rich often make excuses. Their interest lies in business or their own pleasures. They have little hunger for food or the things of God. But the poor will all come and feast.

So, what do the hungry look like in the West? God calls us to the emotionally poor and broken. He sends us to those who are hungry, sick and needy, the old and the forgotten. He sends us to the latchkey children and the fatherless. He sends us to prisoners, felons, the homeless, immigrants, addicts, and those in great pain. Those who know they need help and are desperate for God and hungry for His presence will be satisfied, as this beatitude promises.

Wake Up, Sleeping Beauty

God once gave me profound vision of another wedding feast. There was the most delicious food set out in every direction, as far as the eye could see. The wedding feast was perfectly set and ready, but the church was lulled asleep.

Jesus said, "Wake up, sleeping beauty! Wake up, sleeping beauty." I saw Him kiss His bride on the forehead and wake her up. Then I saw as the Lord Jesus stood on this huge mountain of garbage. There He and I were dancing together among all those with bloated bellies, bruised bodies, and worms coming out of their toes and stomachs.

Jesus and I went around to touch each one. As we laid our hands on them, their bellies became flat. As we touched their feet, their sores closed and healed. Jesus took away their filthy, tattered rags. Then He placed beautiful robes of gold, silver, purple, red, and blue on them.

Everyone arose out of the garbage, singing and dancing, and they followed Jesus into the wedding feast. He showed them the beautiful food and said, "You get to sit in front."

That is the way it should be. No one should have to live outside under a bridge. No one must be required to scavenge in the garbage for something to eat or to wear. No one should be so hungry that they have to live with a bloated belly. No one should starve to death.

But to feast at His table, we need to fully understand who we are, church. Like these African children, we scavenge like orphans when, in fact, the Father has already declared, "I want you. I love you. Come home to My feast. It is time to eat."

People with a Western mind-set think what we have is so bountiful because opportunities abound. We have our favorite snacks and brand-name drinks like orphans—not able to recognize that there is something much better. Pride keeps us from affirming that the poor could have something *we* need.

Come Eat and Drink of Me

> And as they were eating, Jesus took bread, blessed and broke it, and gave it to the disciples and said, "Take, eat; this is My body." Then He took the cup, and gave thanks, and gave it to them, saying, "Drink from it, all of you. For this is My blood of the new covenant, which is shed for many for the remission of sins."
>
> —MATTHEW 26:26–28, NKJV

The poor taught me how to hunger for God and to take spiritual communion. He invites us to eat and to drink of Jesus so that we become full. Just as we depend on food for our physical nourishment, we also need to depend on Jesus for the spiritual nourishment of our lives. We must feed on Him daily. Only then will we have the fresh bread from heaven that we need to give to both the spiritually and naturally hungry.

Out of the abundance of our own feasting at His table, we will have fresh manna from heaven to give to the poor every day. As Mother Teresa once said:

> When Jesus came into the world, He loved it so much that He gave His life for it. He wanted to satisfy our hunger for God. And what did He do? He made Himself the Bread of Life. He became small, fragile, and defenseless for us. Bits of bread can be so small that even a baby can chew it.

He became the Bread of Life to satisfy our
hunger for God, our hunger for love.[1]

After we learn to eat of Him, we will then run into the
darkness with fresh bread for the multitudes. For even the
poor do not like stale bread. We cannot live on yesterday's
manna or old revelation. Often in religious circles people
are offered stale bread to eat, but no one wants it. So we
must press into His presence and be filled with His real,
fresh food every day or we will grow stale.

There is this fullness that Jesus promised: "Blessed are
those who hunger and thirst for righteousness, for they
shall be filled" (Matt. 5:6). The Father has invited all of us
into His wedding feast to sit with Him, to come and eat.
That means no more crumbs, no more stale bread, and no
more garbage. We can just come in, let Him hold us, let
Him love us, and let Him smile on us.

In Mozambique, sometimes when we take the homeless orphans in, they run away and scavenge again in the
dark places. But Jesus always leaves the ninety-nine to
chase after the one. He always searches for the one lost
coin. Jesus kills the fattened calf, throws the best party in
town, and promises, "My son...you are always with me,
and everything I have is yours" (Luke 15:31).

Eat for a Nation

When everything Jesus has is ours, we can start to feed
the nations. Attending a conference is not enough. You
must eat and drink until you are dripping Jesus. You
must be so full of Him that you start leaking Jesus. You
must eat a lot—more than just twice a year. You must eat
enough for a nation.

The poor have taught me about hunger and thirst and my own need. In order to function and to make it through one day, I have to spend hours every day alone with my Jesus. I must have His presence or I know I cannot survive. I am often on my face in His presence. So I stay hidden in His heart, soaking in the secret place. If you will look into the eyes of Jesus and eat and fill that hungry place with Him every day, then His passion is alive and burning in your soul.

When I come up from that secret place, I sometimes watch blind eyes turn from white to gray to brown as King Jesus heals them; I watch thousands of unreached people bow their knees to Jesus. And I watch previously miserable, abandoned children swing on swing sets as they sing joyful songs to the Lord. My life must be one lived out of fullness and abundance. I will never claim to have anything on my own.

Learn to eat and drink from the Word. Fill your hunger and thirst with the Word. Jesus is the Word—the Bread of Life. See Him in the Word, in the poor, and in the face of the hungry ones on the street.

> Come, all you who are thirsty, come to the waters; and you who have no money, come, buy and eat! Come, buy wine and milk without money and without cost. Why spend money on what is not bread, and your labor on what does not satisfy? Listen, listen to me, and eat what is good, and your soul will delight in the richest of fare.
>
> —ISAIAH 55:1–2

Go to Jesus in faith. Look into His eyes and love Him. Be desperate for more of Him. What we don't have, Jesus has, and He is good; He will give to us. His body and blood are more than enough for all who receive Him.

We must keep testifying to the gospel of God's grace, and out of it we will see more revival. We and the rest of the body of Christ will persevere and do greater things than even Jesus did on Earth, things He has prepared for us to do from before the foundation of the world.

Blessed are those who hunger and thirst for righteousness, for they will be filled.

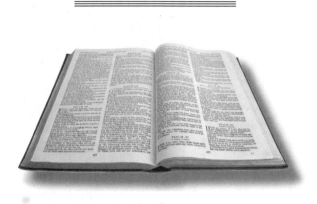

Devotional

The world today is hungry not only for bread but hungry for love; hungry to be wanted, to be loved. They're hungry to feel that presence of Christ. In many countries, people have everything except that presence, that understanding. That's why the life of prayer and sacrifice comes to give that love. By being contemplative, you are to be that presence, that bread of God to break.[2]

—MOTHER TERESA

Five

BLESSED ARE THE MERCIFUL

*At the moment of death we will not be judged
according to the number of good deeds we
have done or by the diplomas we have received
in our lifetime. We will be judged according
to the love we have put into our work.*[1]
—MOTHER TERESA

RECENTLY, WE HAD A DIFFICULT SITUATION where we had hundreds of people left over after a conference. They were brand-new baby Christians. They were hungry and angry, so they began to riot. They all were screaming, and they wanted to fight.

They were yelling, "We're going to burn down the kitchen!" Well, the kitchen wasn't very slick—nothing fancy at all. It was a piece of plastic over some bamboo poles because that was all we had. And we had some wood to make a fire.

I asked God what to do. I knew He could create something from nothing because He is God. It was a very difficult situation. We felt our lives were at stake. But I also knew that God promised to bless those who hunger and thirst for righteousness.

Then I heard God call to me and say, "Step in the middle of the riot."

So I stepped into this angry mob while they were screaming, "We're hungry. Our children are hungry. You're starving us to death. We came to the conference. There's no food!"

That's when I started to cry, and I told them how sorry I was. Then I asked them to please forgive me; it was all I could think to do. This angry mob stopped screaming; they stopped fighting. Looking at me, they said, "We forgive you, Mama Aida."

I thought that was wonderful, but I still needed food to feed everyone. Just then one of our Iris trucks drove up carrying a pot of food. The pot was filled with gooey spaghetti—not the kind of pasta most people in the West would even eat. The kind of spaghetti we have is stuck together in a gooey ball. The problem was that there was only enough spaghetti to feed, at most, about fifty people. But there were more than four hundred people left in the crowd.

There were also about a hundred Westerners who had come to camp out at the conference. I smiled and asked them to serve the food.

They just looked at me. Most of them had heard me speak at a conference, but perhaps they did not really believe the miracles. They asked if I knew how many people were there. I replied, "I read the Book. Serve the food, and please heap their plates full as they are very hungry."

Now, I could have sent the westerners away so they did not have to see the chaos, but I wanted them to see the glory! I told them to watch Jesus.

Those westerners served spaghetti on bread until almost everyone was fed. Then another beautiful miracle happened when one of our long-term missionaries took some of the hungry new believers to her house afterward to feed them. Even the westerners who were brave enough ate our gooey spaghetti too.

Yes, my God is God! We can believe in who He is, and we can believe that He will do what He says He will do.

An Easter Story: Francis Raised From the Dead

One of my favorite stories about God and His mercy involves one of our pastors whose name is Francis. A few years ago we had a regional conference in South Africa. Our conferences are a little different from Western conferences. All our people sleep outside in the dirt or on the floor of the church.

About 4:00 p.m., Pastor Francis went outside to lock the gate and to quiet a gang who had come there to cause trouble. But the gang jumped on him and beat him severely until he died.

When our Pastor Surpresa called the police, they told him, "We're not coming at this time of night. It's too dangerous there." So he called the hospital. The hospital operator replied, "No, we won't send an ambulance to that neighborhood."

No one even had a car available, so finally, Pastor Surpresa was able to borrow an old car from a friend to bring Pastor Francis's body to the hospital. Everyone was praying as the car had to be push started. The whole church was crying out to heaven; Pastor Francis had been dead for more than an hour.

But at 12:15 a.m., while the church was gathered together praying in one accord, Francis came back to life! His whole face and body were swollen, his clothes were shredded, and he was in excruciating pain. The doctors did not know what to do except to give him morphine for the pain. Before he went to sleep from the medicine, through his broken and swollen lips he said just two words: "Forgive them."

Pastor Surpresa went to the hospital at 6:00 a.m. to visit Francis. Pastor Francis's eyes were swollen shut, he was covered with bruises, and his whole body was swollen. He was a tragic mess, and he could hardly think straight or communicate because his lips were swollen. It looked as though he would take a long time to recover.

Meanwhile, the church kept praying and considering what should be done with the gang if the police caught them. Before long it was agreed that according to what Pastor Francis had said, the church would forgive them.

Later in the morning, the police caught one of the gang members. They called the church and asked that someone come and file charges at the police station. Pastor Surpresa told them there was a little problem because the man who had been murdered was no longer dead, and the church decided that no charges would be filed against the gang.

This thoroughly agitated the police, who believed it would only encourage more crime. They wanted the teenager to be jailed for at least eighteen months. But Pastor Surpresa and the church were firm. They believed that mercy triumphs over justice and forgiveness always wins. So, the boy was forgiven and released into the church's custody.

As soon as the decision was made to forgive the young man, Francis's body was totally healed. After matters with the police were resolved, the hospital also called to ask someone to come and pick up Pastor Francis.

Surpresa went to the hospital and found Francis totally well; he had no swelling, bruising, scars, or problems whatsoever. It was as though he had never been attacked the night before. Patients were not allowed to be released on a Sunday at this hospital because they were watched until Monday. But there was nothing wrong with Francis, so they had no reason to keep him.

The only evidence left from the attack was Francis's clothes. Surpresa had to go out and buy new clothes for him because his others were torn to shreds from the beating.

The next morning, Francis himself went to the police station with Surpresa to pick up the teenager. The police were still very angry and said, "Do whatever you want with him."

Remembering Matthew 5:7—"Blessed are the merciful, for they will be shown mercy"—the entire community decided to respond in the opposite spirit, and they ministered to him with deep love and compassion. Within an hour, the boy gave his heart to Jesus. He has since started studying at our Bible college, and he plans to become a pastor.

At our Easter service the same year, Pastor Francis sat on the platform, showing everyone that he was indeed raised from the dead and also about to marry his beloved bride. Rolland and I looked at each other, smiled, and said in agreement, "No one has to preach much. Pastor Francis *is* the message!"

Just think about it: Pastor Francis was back from the dead to marry his bride on Resurrection Sunday! What an awesome illustration of what Jesus did for us! It was such a beautiful day as his bride walked down the aisle, beaming with love and gratitude. They had truly been shown great mercy.

Another man who was affected by bandits on the street was Luis. I remember finding him when he was on the street and very sick. Luis was also angry because the bandits had burned him and his house.

The house Luis considered his home at the time was nothing more than a cardboard box. The bandits had tied rope around his cardboard house while he was sleeping in it, poured gasoline on it, set it on fire, and left him to die. He was terribly burned and had to spend months and months recovering in the dilapidated local hospital. Luis was sick, diseased, and angry that he had been treated so horribly.

In the natural, Luis was not a very merciful person. He made his living by stealing, beating people up, and knifing them. But his misery from being burned brought him to a place of great brokenness. He had nothing left to take pride in. He wet himself, he was filthy, he was angry, and he was broken. I spent time with Luis and became his friend.

Luis was already eighteen years old by then and, according to our rules, too old to come live with us—but I seem to break a few rules!

I told him about this man named Jesus who had given up His home and riches and walked the streets. I described my beautiful Jesus who left heaven and came to Earth to find him. I told him about Jesus's passionate love. Luis said, "I must know this man." I told him that this man lives inside of me.

Things didn't change very quickly for Luis, but instead

remained very difficult. We gave him new clothes and a home and tried to show him mercy. One day, Luis came to me and said, "Mama Aida, I am going to come with you to the street and tell those guys who tried to kill me that I forgive them."

After he forgave those who tried to burn him to death, he continued to pour out great mercy as he ministered to others on the streets. And I watched the kindness of God pour through Luis's life.

The Fragrance of Jesus to a Broken and Dying World

One of our churches at that time was an unconventional congregation in an unconventional place. We met in a brothel so that we could reach the prostitutes there. We would worship Jesus, pray, and simply love the resident prostitute girls. But we were not seeing a lot of break-through. The girls were not able to escape from their destructive lifestyles.

I was so desperate for Jesus to set these girls free that I went on a forty-day fast. I was very hungry. In my hunger and desperation, I cried out, "God, You have got to do something! You have to change this situation so that they do not sell their bodies anymore." I asked God to change the hearts of these girls—some of them were ten-, eleven-, and twelve-year-olds going into the streets to sell their bodies for a bottle of cola.

Then one day as I drove up to the brothel where I was about to hold a church service, the girls ran toward me. They were screaming, "We cannot sell ourselves anymore. We want to give up prostitution."

I started weeping, and they fell on their knees to worship God during the service.

I prayed, asking God what I should do next. I knew that I could not move these girls into the same center as the boys. I had to plant a church and find a pastor whose heart matched Jesus's—in holiness and purity but without judgment.

An Unlikely Candidate

After crying out to God, I looked up. There was a man praying and worshiping God in the dirt. It was Luis. He hadn't been able to finish the pastors' Bible school because he could not read or write. But he was a man full of mercy.

There in the dirt, Luis was worshiping God. His hands were lifted up, and he was adoring the Lord. I knelt down and asked him if he would like to pastor these girls.

He fell apart, sobbing. Then he looked up at me and asked, "Would God give me that privilege and such a beautiful thing to do? Would Jesus honor me with such a task? Could His great love use a man like me?"

Luis had gained great humility and great love, so he accepted the position as pastor, moved to a small new base, and pastored those girls.

This was the only church I ever planted that I one day chose to close. But I really had no choice. We had to move out of the brothel because all the girls left their life of prostitution!

Luis is in heaven now. He died of the AIDS that he contracted in his youth while living on the streets. But God continued to send more wonderful heroes to care for those girls.

Luis's life was a life of love poured out before his King. I know that today in heaven, Luis is full of joy with his Bridegroom.

Another Unlikely Heroine—Helena

Another heroine of mine who taught me about mercy is named Helena. Though she only had one leg, Helena's life was truly blessed. She taught me about the blessing of extending mercy and living a life embodying the Beatitudes.

One day we were in Maputo, just sitting on the street, when suddenly I heard gunshots. The police were shooting at and trying to kill some kids who had been stealing.

Then I heard a boy screaming, "Mama Aida, they are trying to kill me. Please protect me." He had stolen a car.

I told him, "Of course I will protect you." And I cried out to God, "Jesus, save him. Don't let him die." I remember the boy was terrified as I held him in my arms. He had already been shot in the arm, and he was bleeding. Later that night, we took him to the local hospital.

Meanwhile, at a distance, Helena watched me as I held this boy in my arms. She tried to hide the tears that were rolling down her cheeks until she hobbled over to where I sat with him.

I asked her if she would like to talk. I could tell that she had been greatly touched by the entire incident. I'm not sure how old either Helena or the boy were—after a life of being abandoned on the streets, they had no idea themselves. The one-legged girl sat to the right, and the young boy who had a gunshot wound in his arm was to my left.

I asked Helena why she only had one leg. She told me she had been burned in a fire. Since her leg was burned off, her family thought she would no longer be of any use. So her grandmother took her outside and told her brothers to kill her. The brothers took her to a field, threw rocks at her, and left her there to die.

Helena said she was filled with anger. She would scream and roll on the ground. She wanted to see her family dead. But God sent a man who, like the good Samaritan, saw her in the field, stopped to help her, and took her to a hospital, and she stayed there for nine months.

We do not know how she managed to stay alive at the hospital in Mozambique because the hospital there does not feed you. If your family or someone you know does not bring you food, you do not have anything to eat. She was just left there in that hospital alone with very little food for nine months.

Helena was then forced to be another little girl who had to sell her body for food to eat. Was this justice? It was not the love of God. How could this happen?

After a little while, I was able to speak to Helena about a Man who would look at her with pure eyes. I told her that this Man would think she was beautiful— that Man is Christ Jesus, who gave up His life for her. Helena received Jesus right there in the streets before she came home to live with us at our children's center.

Those Who Are Forgiven Much, Love Much

At first, Helena still talked about how she hated her family for trying to kill her. As she grew in love with Jesus, she also grew in mercy. The love of God flowing through that girl just amazed me. We were able to get her a makeshift prosthetic leg, and after a few months, she came to me and told me she wanted to go home. She wanted to go and tell her brothers about Jesus, and she wanted her grandmother to meet Him too.

I was really concerned, though, knowing how difficult her family background was. But when you know you are truly forgiven, you then learn how to forgive. Jesus, when speaking about a woman whose sins had been great, challenged His disciples by saying, "I tell you, her many sins have been forgiven—for she loved much. But he who has been forgiven little loves little" (Luke 7:47).

Helena, who had been full of hatred and anger, received God's mercy and forgiveness. Even if her family killed her when she went back home, she was determined to show mercy to them and let the light of Jesus shine.

When she got home, she led one of her brothers into a relationship with Jesus. Her grandmother, however, continued to be a witch doctor. Helena moved into a small reed hut that was next to her family's home and continued to love them. Her life of pain and prostitution was over.

I remember when I performed her wedding sometime later. I recall as she walked down the aisle of our church toward her bridegroom. She wore a dress that had been worn by others many times before, but she looked stunning, purified, and filled with radiant joy. She had truly been forgiven of much.

She had poured out great mercy to her family, and she received great mercy from God in return. God blessed her with a wedding, a family, and beautiful children of her own. She also forgave everyone who had abused her.

But—a very important part—she forgave herself and let the hatred and rage go. So, she was able to receive the mercy of God and poured His mercy out on all those around her.

*Blessed are the merciful, for
they will receive mercy.*

Devotional

Dear Lord:

Help me to spread your fragrance wherever I go.

Flood my soul with your spirit and life.

Penetrate and possess my whole being so utterly that all my life may only be a radiance of yours.

Shine through me, and be so in me that every soul I come in contact with may feel your presence in my soul.

Let them look up and see no longer me, but only you, O Lord!

Stay with me, then I shall begin to shine as you do; so to shine as to be a light to others.

The light, O Lord, will be all from you; none of it will be mine; it will be you shining on others through me.

Let me thus praise you in the way you love best, by shining on those around me.

Let me preach you without preaching, not by words but by my example, by the catching force, the sympathetic influence of what I do, the evident fullness of the love my heart bears to you.

Amen.[2]

—JOHN HENRY NEWMAN
(ONE OF MOTHER TERESA'S FAVORITE PRAYERS,
SAID EVERY DAY BY THE MISSIONARIES OF CHARITY)

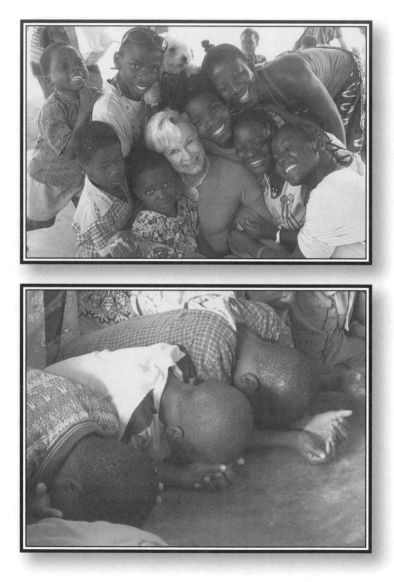

Six

BLESSED ARE THE PURE IN HEART

*It is not necessary to always be meditating,
nor to consciously experience the sensa-
tion that we are talking to God, no matter
how nice this would be. What matters is
being with Him, living in Him, in His will.*[1]
—MOTHER TERESA

W HEN I MEDITATE ON HOW GOD INTENDED us to be "pure in heart," I think on the words of Mother Teresa: "Our vocation, to be beautiful, must be full of thought for others."[2] And, "To love with a pure heart, to love everybody, especially to love the poor, is a twenty-four-hour prayer."[3]

Loving the poor is truly a full-time job, but it is one filled with tremendous joy. I am daily challenged when the needs are so great, the queues so long, and the multitudes so hungry. Among the poor in Africa, we are seeing revival fueled and sustained by the power of God in spite of all our weaknesses. His mercies and compassions never fail; they are new every morning.

> We have this treasure in jars of clay to show that this all-surpassing power is from God and not from us. We are hard pressed on every side, but not crushed; perplexed, but

not in despair; persecuted, but not abandoned; struck down, but not destroyed. We
always carry around in our body the death
of Jesus, so that the life of Jesus may also be
revealed in our body.

—2 CORINTHIANS 4:7–10

When I think of what God requires to be pure in heart,
I think of my beautiful Mozambican children. These children are my delight as they hunger for more of Jesus. They
are my mentors, and they have helped to teach me not
to be led astray from the simplicity and purity of devotion. Sometimes we make things too complicated when
we really need to remember that the kingdom belongs to
the children!

We pray for fresh bread from heaven every day. And
God has been giving some of our pastors and children
heavenly visitations and visions.

Crispen

During a Friday night chapel service, one of our boys,
Crispen, who was about twelve years old, had a vision
while worshiping the Lord. Suddenly he had the vivid
experience of something very dark flying out of his heart.
He then saw a brilliant white light come into his heart
and explode. Then he heard a voice say, "We are more
than conquerors."

Crispen came to me and asked if I knew what it meant.
He was undone by the Holy Spirit; tears were streaming
down his face.

This visitation could not have come at a better time.
We were exhausted, overextended, and overrun by needs,

crises, corruption, disappointment, and the desperate cry for relief that rises up constantly from the world of the poor. Crispen's childlike faith and heart showed us God's perspective even in the midst of great battle.

We choose to keep God's perspective. We will not concentrate on weaknesses in ourselves or the dark forces of danger on all sides, but rather on His face. We are sustained by beholding the beauty of His gaze, and we are confident in His cross—His gospel is sufficient. Crispen was right: we are more than conquerors through Him who loves us!

We knelt down in the dirt beside Crispen and asked him to pray for us. As the tears rolled down his brown cheeks, he worshiped God. Crispen had been with us for six months. He had just received Jesus and had no biblical understanding for what he was experiencing.

During this visitation, an American visitor came over to pray and prophesy over my personal assistant, Shara. She started prophesying in English, seeing a vision of how God was giving Shara new armor.

Crispen was in a heavenly vision, not understanding a word of the visitor's English prayer. Then he sweetly turned to Shara, who was facedown in the dirt, and described to her the exact prophetic word, but in Portuguese. Two people, two generations, two continents, two languages, but the same God. Crispen's prophetic word encouraged us to press onward in Christ Jesus.

Seeing the children experience heaven is a sign to me that the glory of the Lord will cover the earth as the waters cover the sea (Hab. 2:14). Today, God's love for the orphan and widow is flooding over Mozambique as so many run to Jesus. Through these children who are pure in heart, I watch Him call the poor into the wedding feast. They teach me to stay hidden in God's heart and to be fully possessed by His sweet presence.

We can only find rest in the secret place of God's heart. Here we will lie down and we will listen until God tells us to stand up. But when we do stand up, whole nations will run to Jesus.

These visitations have provoked me to want to live continually in the Ezekiel 47 river. I want to be fully immersed in His glory, to see His eyes, to touch His heart, and to give away His ceaseless, limitless, bottomless love to a lost and dying world. Only when we are completely yielded will nations come to Him.

Children's Key: Purity of the Heart

And now, little children, abide in Him, that when He appears, we may have confidence and not be ashamed before Him at His coming....Behold what manner of love the Father has bestowed on us, that we should be called children of God! Therefore the world does not know us, because it did not know Him. Beloved, now we are children of God; and it has not yet been revealed what we shall be, but we know that when He is revealed, we shall be like Him, for we shall see Him as He is.

—1 JOHN 2:28; 3:1–2, NKJV

When He appears, we shall be like Him! We shall see as He sees and feel as He feels. But we do not have to wait until we get to heaven to let Him purify us. We must cry out to be purified and freed from every hidden agenda, rotten motive, and false assumption about God.

My heart's one desire is to be holy in love. I long for the purifying fire of His love to consume every hidden motive within me. As the heart is purified, we can see Him with greater and greater clarity. I want to be fully possessed by His Holy Spirit until I am completely overshadowed by God. I want to be utterly overtaken.

My prayer is for all of us to stay hidden inside God's glorious heart of love until we are manifesting His nature as sons and daughters, living, breathing, moving, healing, and life giving, just as Jesus was. As we are purified, we will see God more clearly. As our hearts become pure, our vision becomes clearer.

The Fire of His Eyes

Set me as a seal upon your heart, as a seal upon your arm; for love is as strong as death, jealousy as cruel as the grave; its flames are flames of fire, a most vehement flame. Many waters cannot quench love, nor can the floods drown it.

—SONG OF SOLOMON 8:6–7, NKJV

Every time I have had a heavenly vision, I have been undone by Jesus's eyes of love. They are like liquid flames of fiery love. And as that scripture just said, many waters cannot quench this love.

Beloved, we are called to focus on His heart. If we have the courage to focus on His face and lock our gazes with Him, He will purify our hearts. When He looks into us with His eyes like a flame of fire, eternity is branded on our hearts. Once we behold His face, we become more like Him, and then we can dwell in the fire of His embrace.

Isaiah 33:14–15 says, "'Who among us shall dwell

with everlasting burnings?' He who walks righteously..."
(NKJV). To dwell in this fire, we must fix our eyes on
Jesus. Then, when people peer into our eyes, Jesus is the
one who looks back at them.

I believe God wants to pour out a fresh salve to give
us His eyes to see and His ears to hear a lost and dying
world. Our God has been made too small in our eyes; we
imagine that He has limits.

We must have pure eyes and pure hearts to see God
for who He truly is. When we don't have His eyes, we
start to see God in our own image rather than seeing
humanity in the image of God. We must know that He
is big enough for all our needs. When we see with God's
perspective, it is so much bigger than our own.

Recently I had another visitation. I was picked up by
two angels, one on each side, and we began to fly across
the nations of the earth. The angels handed me some
golden oil as I saw multitudes of sick, dying, and broken
people. I flew with the angels over nations and poured
out this golden oil like honey on the people.

They all fell on their faces, and everyone was healed. I
saw this huge, incredible harvest like nothing I had ever
seen before. But we are now beginning to experience this
harvest and the fulfillment of that vision. And we are seeing
that God's heart is big enough to love the entire world.

Arsenio

Another one of my Mozambican sons, Arsenio, had a
vision of Jesus's face that expanded his capacity to love.
Arsenio is a picture for me of how God can purify our
hearts. He is a half-caste child whom I found dying in the

trash. He was trying to survive by scavenging from one of the world's poorest garbage dumps.

Arsenio was full of demons. As a small child, he could easily throw several pastors off himself. I did not know anything else to do for him but to hold him in my arms and pray quietly for his heart to be healed. Arsenio was set free. I knew that there was something very special about this little boy.

One day as we were worshiping in our church tent in Zimpeto, I watched as Arsenio lay facedown in the sand, sobbing and worshiping God. He was crying and shaking—he was desperate for God. Hour after hour, our Mozambican aunties who oversee the children were getting more and more nervous. They finally came to me as I was preaching and said, "Mama Aida, what should we do?"

I said, "It's good what's happening to him. I understand because I have been on the floor myself for days at a time. I know what it means to be there. His weeping is a sign of a holy visitation. Leave him alone there; God is touching him."

Of all the children whom God could have chosen, He had handpicked this little one—the one most broken, the most hungry, who loved God with all his heart.

Arsenio forgave his parents, who had abandoned him. But he was desperate for a father. And our Father God came and met his pure heart as Arsenio lay there on the ground, broken and worshiping Jesus.

At the end of the evening, we picked him up because he was unable to move. We carried him back to his room, laid him on his bed, and tucked his quilt around him, blessing him. I leaned over, kissed his cheek, and said, "I'll see you tomorrow." But he still could not speak.

The next day as I was playing with the little girls, Arsenio saw me and came bolting toward me. When he jumped into my arms, I said, "You are absolutely radiant!"

He said, "Mama Aida, I saw Jesus!"

Then I asked him why he was crying. Arsenio said he was weeping over the sins of Mozambique. He told me that Jesus said, "All who come to Me, I will forgive."

"I Saw Jesus"

Today Arsenio shares the good news from a flatbed truck with the poor who live in the bush. He is so full of life and light. When he looks out on a crowd of even a thousand or more in an unreached people group, he is not intimidated. Although his heart still aches for his lost parents, since that visitation he knows he is not an orphan but a son of the house. He knows signs and wonders are not reserved for the spiritual elite.

The heart of the Father beats inside of Arsenio as he preaches with joy. He sings and worships God, and when people throw stones at him, he does not care. When he lays hands on the sick, they are often healed.

I have watched as that child who was once the most rejected now lives with the light of God's glory and burns brightly with the fire of God's love. And I have watched him work through painful issues by the grace of God. Something happened during that visitation that increased Arsenio's capacity to love and forgive. God took his heart of stone and gave him a heart of flesh (Ezek. 36:26).

Arsenio was just a little boy—a little castaway, hidden boy who wept over the many sins of Mozambique. No one seemed to know him, but Jesus knew him. Jesus told him, "All who come to Me, I will forgive." Now Arsenio can believe for a nation because he has seen the face of God.

Spirit of Adoption

And he said to him, "Son, you are always
with me, and all that I have is yours."
—LUKE 15:31, NKJV

If we are childlike, we will know God as our Father and see Him as He is. I have a tradition in Mozambique; I never call our children's centers, like our center in Pemba that we call the Village of Joy, "orphanages," because the children are no longer orphans. We see them as ones who have been adopted by their Father in heaven.

Once while in a church in Canada, I was actually stuck to the floor for seven days and seven nights. During this time, Rolland read to me from the Book of Ephesians while God gave me a major revelation about sonship and told me to take in every dying child He placed before us.

Taking in thousands and thousands of orphaned and abandoned children has taught us so much about the nature of the Father heart of God. Just as the father promises in Luke 15, all that God has is ours for the receiving of our inheritance.

God has blessed us in the heavenly realm with every blessing in Christ Jesus (Eph. 1:4). We were chosen and handpicked and have full access to the heavenly realm because of the finished work of the cross. This is a key for accessing the heavenly realms by faith.

Your Picture Is on God's Fridge

I do not think it was just Arsenio's purity of heart that made him so irresistible to God; it was also his childlike faith. I believe he understands the spirit of adoption and the seal of the Holy Spirit and that he can run forward in faith to his Father in heaven with no fear of rejection. Arsenio is completely adored by us, he has been taken into our family, and he knows what it means to be adopted by his heavenly Father too.

It is an orphan spirit that causes people to shrink back, peer around the corners, and not believe that there is room enough on their Father God's lap. When we first take in children from the street, they are usually little bandits whose bodies are full of lice and scabies, and they are generally really rotten rascals.

They are not nice, sweet little children! They are not cuddly little angels. But we welcome them with open arms into our villages. On the weekends, we have sleepovers with eight of our children who have been with us for years and eight of our new children. At first, the new ones are so timid that they won't even eat anything from the fridge. They feel that they have to work for what they want—or they have to steal it. The children who know who they are with us open the fridge and help themselves to everything!

The new children do not yet understand that they were chosen before the foundation of the world; they were predestined to be God's children. They do not yet understand His grace or know that they were adopted as sons through Jesus Christ in accordance with His pleasure and will (Eph. 1).

They are still afraid, and they often steal or think they must earn everything and strive for acceptance. They have to learn about adoption into God's family and then trust that they really are wanted. It is a delight to see when they really have a true experience of adoption. They truly do change and find joy! This can only happen as a gift of the Holy Spirit.

The spirit of adoption means we were hand chosen by our heavenly Father. With that choosing comes our rights as sons and daughters of our Father. Let me offer you an illustration. I have two children, Elisha and Crystalyn. I did not get to pick them; I gave birth to them, but I think they are absolutely awesome. I never say, "Hey, I wish you were more like..." No, they are flesh of my flesh and truly amazing people. They make my heart sing. But when we adopt children, we actually go out and look for them—we choose them.

After fourteen years of ministering to children in the streets and villages of Mozambique, I am beginning to understand more about the spirit of adoption. God is looking for spiritual fathers and mothers who know who they are in Him, who will go into the darkness, look for lost children (spiritual orphans) of all ages, and bring them home to the Father's house.

Our attempts to minister to others may be feeble to some, but they are precious to God. We may minister like a three-year-old drawing their first picture, but we try as hard as we can, and with great joy we scribble our picture for God. We may mess it up or rip the page. But when God our Father looks at what we have done for Him, He says, "It's amazing; it's fabulous!" If God had a fridge in heaven, our pictures would be on it.

As the Father heals the abandoned and orphaned spirits of these children, they start realizing that the kingdom is theirs too. The children who once stole from us are now totally transformed and are leaders at the new children's villages. They no longer have to hide in the shadows and sneak around; their hearts have been made pure by God, and now they have seen His goodness.

From Servant to Son; From Orphan to Heir

Ramadan is another one of our Mozambican children. When he first came to us, he would run around and bite and kick people, looking miserable all the time. Ramadan had experienced great pain in his early childhood and had never known love. He had been raised in a Muslim family, and both of his parents had died. There was so much shame and sadness in him that he would not look anyone in the eye. Ramadan did not think he had access to Rolland, to me, or to our family.

Like some of the other children, Ramadan could not comprehend what a fridge was because he had never seen one before. He would not dare move to go toward the fridge, and he had never had a Coca-Cola in his life. So, I took Ramadan by the hand and told him, "That fridge has a Coke in it. You can go get that Coke whenever you want it." I also said, "Ramadan, I'm going to tuck you in and sing you a song. I will look you in the eyes, and I will love you."

Then God started transforming his little heart.

We are all a bit like this with God. We think things like, "Am I really allowed? Can I really open that door and drink of Him? Does He really love me?" But over time, God heals our abandoned and orphaned spirits.

Finally, one day Ramadan walked up to that fridge and took the drink. The first time he opened the fridge door and realized that he belonged to the family, joy hit his heart and spiked across his face. He realized that he had full access to the house.

All that is in God's house is available to His sons and daughters too. We are allowed to partake of His peace, His joy, His patience, His long-suffering, His healing, and His provision. We are free to be intimate with Him and walk into the secret place as a son or daughter.

Welcome Home

Many of us are like Ramadan because we have access to the heavenly realm, but we are not sure whether the Father wants to see us. Some wonder whether there is a God who is near or if He actually hears us. Others think that God does hear them but that He does not want to answer them. First John 4:18 tells us, "There is no fear in love. But perfect love drives out fear, because fear has to do with punishment. The one who fears is not made perfect in love."

Most of us stand at the fridge door, wondering if God is going to slap our hands if we dare to open it and feast in the Father's house. Or we think that God is low on Cokes and wants to save them for the special children—or at least save them for some other time when we are really good. So, we timidly step away from God. This is the orphan spirit.

Orphans compete with each other, always comparing and worrying that there is not enough, worrying that if God blesses someone else, they will miss out. Sons and daughters of God who are pure in heart give preference to each other, knowing that there is always enough in the Father's house.

So, when God welcomes you home, taking away your

orphaned spirit and giving you a pure spirit of sonship, you can boldly come forward, realizing that a loving Father declares, "Everything I have is yours" (Luke 15:31). The Father loves you!

Orphan Spirit in the Western World

We want to be pure in heart. We want to see God as He is. Sometimes, though, in the Western culture of individualism and ambitious drive, we more easily fall into the trap of the orphan spirit. We look around and think that the Father loves one person more than another according to how blessed they are.

That's when envy, competition, strife, and jealousy creep in. We compare and compete, and then we fight with each other. We see God as a hard taskmaster whose love for us is based on our performance.

My two natural-born children, Elisha and Crystalyn, are very different from each other. You would not expect them to have been born of the same parents. Their giftings and anointings are so unalike, but they both are wonderfully and uniquely made. We do not like one better than the other. We think they are both absolutely perfect. They both delight our hearts. I never look at Christy and ask her to be more like Elisha; we do not ask Elisha to be like Christy—or anyone else. They are ours, and we love them the way they are.

Sometimes when we act like orphans, it's because we think God wants us to be like someone else. Some think, "Look at that guy preaching in a stadium. God must love him more!" But to God, when we are covered in the blood of Jesus, we are all beautiful. All of God's children are equally beautiful because we are made in His image.

Just to visit Elisha and Crystalyn, who are studying in the United States, we have to fly halfway around the world. It takes three days of travel for a hug! But that is our great delight because our children are our treasures. They are worth everything to us.

The Father is not looking at us and saying, "You have only fasted for thirty-two days. Perhaps on day thirty-eight you can have access to the heavenly realm. I will only love you when you become more like Me."

No, God loved us when we were yet sinners. We cannot earn any more of His love; we cannot lose His love. We have all of His affections. Now we can just rest as true sons and daughters and see all that the Father offers is ours. He is our Papa God. We can see Him as He is. He purifies us by grace!

He Doesn't Just Love You; He Likes You Too

I would never tell my kids to go three weeks without eating before I would talk to them. Fasting does not cause us to gain more favor from God. We fast to be more hungry for Him, not to twist His arm.

My kids always have access to me. They are always welcome with arms wide open into my kitchen. My Mozambican kids often bound into my house on the weekends and eat everything in sight. The same is true with the heavenly realm. God promises that we have been chosen, predestined, conformed to His image, and set apart for His plan. We are vessels of honor created to bring Him glory.

When we start to realize that we are loved, we let go of the things of the world that so easily entangle us. His love purifies us. The purer we become, the more we see Him and the less we hold on to the things of the world.

Jesus knew He could do everything that He saw the Father doing. The same is true for us as sons and daughters on Earth. We are promised to do even greater works than He did.

He stands like a proud papa in heaven, telling us, "You are welcome in My house! All that is Mine is yours. See Me as I am—your heavenly Father!"

Start Living in the Heavenly Realm

So, how do you start seeing Jesus? When you move from orphan to servant to son or daughter and start to understand just how much He delights in you, your life will be completely transformed. Out of the abundance of the overflow of this revelation, you will bound forward to the Father and start living in the heavenly realms.

You have to believe that you are welcome in the Father's house. Provision is your inheritance. All that Jesus died for is waiting for you to take. You do not have to wait until you die to experience heaven on Earth. We are called to live in the fullness of what each precious drop of blood purchased. Start feasting now. True riches are His presence. My greatest treasure is to see the lost children come home to the Father's house. You are called to the feast of Jesus. You are called to be sons and daughters of the Most High God!

***Blessed are the pure in heart,
for they will see God.***

Devotional

Mother Teresa was frequently asked how she managed to face the overwhelming needs day after day. She said:

> My secret is very simple: I pray. Through prayer I become one in love with Christ.[4]

> Prayer is not asking. Prayer is putting oneself in the hands of God, at His disposition, and listening to His voice in the depths of our hearts.[5]

Another time, Mother Teresa answered the same question slightly differently:

> Love to pray.... Prayer enlarges the heart until it is capable of containing God's gift of Himself. Ask and seek and your heart will grow big enough to receive Him as your own.[6]

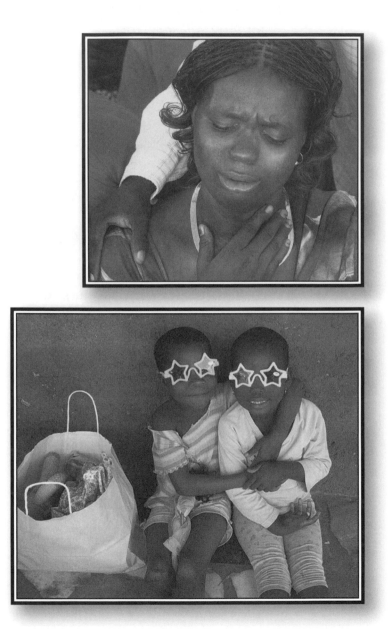

Seven

BLESSED ARE THE PEACEMAKERS

We know only too well that what we are doing is nothing more than a drop in the ocean. But if the drop were not there, the ocean would be missing something.[1]
—MOTHER TERESA

WHAT IS A PEACEMAKER? PEACEMAKERS ARE THE mercy of God to a sinful world. They embody His very kindness.

Rejoice and Be Glad

Blessed are you when people insult you, persecute you and falsely say all kinds of evil against you because of me. Rejoice and be glad, because great is your reward in heaven, for in the same way they persecuted the prophets who were before you.

—MATTHEW 5:11–12

When I meditate on what it means to be a peacemaker, I think of the time we spent south of Mozambique when we had trouble with the government leaders of our children's village.

In 1996–1997, the persecution we experienced in

southern Mozambique reached its highest peak. The government wrote seven slanderous lies about us, accusing us of all manner of evil. Only one item bore truth: we were baptizing people in dirty, polluted water because we had no running water.

The government thought we were rebels trying to bring them down. Much of the opposition to the new free government had been fueled by white South Africa, and some by the United States. So one might be able to understand the concern. The government, as well as fellow churches in the area, had told us to work with educated children instead of these bandits and thieves. They said our children would never amount to anything.

One day the government abruptly came to us and gave us forty-eight hours to completely leave the children's center. I remember looking at our children in what seemed to be a hopeless situation. We were so poor at the time that every day we had to pray for a miracle to feed our 320 children. I told the children to pray, to forgive, and to try to make peace with the government workers.

We had very few resources, and our small staff was exhausted. We would go to our empty warehouse, stand there, pray, and worship. Each night, government workers would clear out what little food we had. Our staff had dwindled because of the persecution and all the difficulties.

One day, we had nearly nothing—in the warehouse we had only ketchup and herbal tea. I thought, "What am I going to do with this? Maybe we could put it on sticks and the children could lick the ketchup off the sticks so at least their stomachs would not be empty."

The Lord led us to worship. At that time, machine-gun

fire was so strong at night that we could hardly sleep. We were desperate with hundreds of hungry children.

I walked into the warehouse and pulled together a few people who believed God to be God, and we worshiped Him together in spite of the circumstances. In God's presence I just fell apart. I said, "God, I love You." I worshiped until I no longer saw an empty warehouse. I kept praising God until all the needs faded away. All I could think of was what a privilege it was to give my life away for love's sake. After hours of worshiping, I closed the warehouse with no dinner or food in sight.

Several hours later, a big truck pulled up. They had to drive on a dirt road with huge potholes filled with muddy water. We were twenty-seven kilometers from the city. I do not know how that truck reached us when it was not even a four-wheel drive. They asked me if I was Mama Aida. When I replied yes, much to my surprise, they told me the food in their truck was for me.

The truck was packed full of cornmeal, rice, beans, and sugar. They just started giving us food. Glory to the Lamb! I did not know who they were or where they had come from. They were Mozambicans, but that was the only time I ever saw them. They never came back. They were like angels in disguise. God did a beautiful miracle for us. Our children started singing and dancing and thanking God for His provision.

You can be truly blessed when you are persecuted. Great is your reward in heaven. You truly are blessed when you choose peace in the midst of war.

We spoke peace to those who wanted us to fight with them. We chose to stay in a place of peace. If you stand, worship, and love God in the midst of lack and difficulty, you will never lose. Jesus always wins. Even if we die for Him, He wins. And in that, we win too.

Fleeing for Our Lives

There was an occasion when we had to escape in the middle of the night so that we would not be killed. We had two trucks at the time—one we named Lazarus because we had to pray for it to be raised each time we wanted to drive it.

At two o'clock in the morning, with a death warrant out for my life, Rolland and I took our two children, Elisha and Crystalyn, and as many small children as we could fit in the trucks. We drove out in the darkness to our little office in downtown Maputo. Two of my missionary heroes, Rachel from the UK and Alison from Australia, were saints as they prayed for God to keep us safe the whole time. They helped us in every way.

All I could pray was, "God, You have to take care of them. I don't know what to do or where to go." We all spoke peace to our persecutors, asking God to *teach them how to love.*

The government came the next morning to threaten the children who remained at the center. They ordered the children to stop worshiping. But our children defied them! They worshiped, they danced, and they sang, thanking Jesus for everything.

This infuriated the atheist government workers. They said every manner of evil against us. They threw rocks at our children and screamed, "You children, if you want food, you will shut your mouths right now! You are not to worship God. If you worship Him, you will die of hunger. We are willing to take over this center if you stop worshiping God. God does not exist. If you read your Bible, if you pray, you will starve to death."

Give Thanks Always

The children looked at them and sang all the louder. Not one child left. The government people were infuriated, so they changed what they were saying and promised the children a home, food, and an education if they would deny their faith and stay behind at my old center, which the government had now confiscated.

In spite of the temptation, not even one child stayed. The children responded in the opposite spirit. The children spoke peace to them. The children knew they were true sons and daughters of God, and their Father in heaven would take care of them.

They all took off, walking twenty-seven kilometers down a dirt road—most of them were barefoot. All of our children, every one of them, came to our little office, singing worship songs in their native Shangaan language.

None of us knew what to do.

They came to the little office building where we were staying in the center of Maputo. We only had two toilets. Our little office room was lined wall to wall with people. Their feet were bloody, their hearts were traumatized, and they had been ridiculed and told that God does not exist.

But they truly were peacemakers! They knew God was their Father. They overcame through a love that never fails. Even if their lives had been taken from them, they would never stop worshiping Jesus! These were not some famous church leaders. They were children without shoes who had been beaten up and persecuted but who refused to forsake the gospel.

They were told they were just street children—without intelligence, without worth, and without any hope in the world. These children stood up to those leaders who threatened their lives, and they walked in peace.

In the face of evil, our children showed mercy. In the face of hatred, they demonstrated Jesus's kindness. In the midst of persecution, they did not fight back, but they embodied what it means to be a peacemaker. Truly they are the sons and daughters of God.

Love Is Always Enough

I felt angry. I did not understand why God would give us 320 children and then allow them to be beaten up and made homeless. I knew theologically that Father God loved us and loved these children, but I surely did not understand how to be a peacemaker in the midst of it all.

I remember looking into the faces of the children one by one, trying to think what would bring them hope. Since the first day I had picked them up from the streets, I had taught the children, "We must love without limit. We will love without end."

A friend of mine named Manessa, who had been a soldier during the war, was very protective of me. One day, when a twenty-dollar contract was put out on my life, he came to me and said, "Don't worry, Mama Aida. I have a plan!" He promised to protect me. He told me he had an AK-47 and a grenade under his bed. He said, "I will go and kill them for you."

Manessa thought I would be very happy to hear of his offer to me, but I turned to him and said, "We are here to love and to bring peace."

I made a decision to go back to the center in broad

daylight. I knew about the danger to my life, but I wanted to speak to my village friends about love and forgiveness. I shared my heart with them and told them, "I want you to love those who want to kill us. I want you to love them without limit and without end. I want you to make peace with them."

My message will never change. All I have to give is love, and this was one of our tests of love.

We could have left and gone to America to escape all the craziness. We could have gone to the international press and fought our case, but we kept hearing the Lord call us to love and forgive. To encourage me in this difficult time, Rolland printed Bible verses and pasted them on the wall. I thought my life was over for a while. I had not eaten or slept for days. Our hearts were broken. Our spirits were crushed. We needed a miracle from heaven.

To answer our prayers, God came and did the first multiplication miracle that I had ever seen. He brought a lady from Texas to our office. She had made chili and rice in a pot to feed our family of four.

I opened the door with nearly a hundred children in the yard, and she got a bit of a shock. She was stunned when she saw the size of our family. She cried, "I made the chili for a family of four." I told her I had a big family and not to worry.

So I looked at her and asked her simply to pray. This upset her; she wanted to go home and cook more. So, she halfheartedly prayed, "God bless it. Amen!"

I am not sure I felt like a peacemaker just then, but I still knew I was a daughter. I think I was too hungry and tired to know what I was doing, so I told the children to sit on the grass mats and get ready for dinner by worshiping Jesus. At the time I did not know that God multiplied plastic plates too, but we had enough in our office. One of our Mozambican daughters, Rabia, and our co-worker friend, Maria, helped serve everyone from a little pot of rice, cornmeal, and chili. I asked them to give the children big helpings because they were very hungry.

In the end, every child ate! For the first time in my life, I saw that there is always enough. God indeed provided for His children in our time of great need.

For Sons of God, Nothing Is Impossible

When we were experiencing this persecution, we prayed daily for our persecutors who put the contract out on my life. God heard our cries! We have since opened three primary schools.

Years later, the government apologetically came into my office repenting after seeing the remarkably high test scores of our children. They came because our children scored the highest in the nation. With tears in their eyes, they asked us to forgive them for confiscating all the buildings. Our children chose to be peacemakers, and they were rewarded greatly.

To me, these children are treasures from heaven. I pray that I will never give up on any child. I am determined to watch and see what Jesus does through their little lives wholly given to Him. Jesus transformed these forgotten children into leaders.

Just recently we heard great news! There are very few universities in Mozambique, and there were more than twelve thousand applications for only two spaces left at one of those respected universities. Both of those spaces were filled with our Iris Mozambican workers. Truly our children will be the future leaders of Mozambique, for they have learned to forgive and to respond in love.

Responding in the Opposite Spirit

Like our children fleeing from their oppressors, we are truly blessed of God, even if it does not always appear so according to the standards of worldly success. To love in the midst of pain, to forgive in the midst of evil, to comfort in the midst of agony, to bring peace in a time of war is the heart of God.

True happiness flows from responding in the opposite spirit of what is expected by the world's standards. Love never fails, and if you remain in love, you will always win.

We continue to experience great spiritual warfare in Mozambique, but we find that the fruit of the Spirit are our ultimate weapon of warfare. Rolland always reminds me that God's workmanship is superb. God knows how to glorify Himself and to protect His honor and reputation in this world. His will is spectacular, joyous, and beyond improvement. His kingdom is the home of righteousness and perfection. His purposes will be accomplished in the earth.

God is thrilled with the progress of His church and where she is going. The dust, chaff, and residual sin of this world do not bring Him down. He is not discouraged or at a loss. He is not just hoping for better things from us, but He is powerfully at work in us—and He will succeed! He will make us into peacemakers, and His kingdom will come with righteousness, peace, and joy in the Holy Spirit (Rom. 14:17).

Sons and Daughters on Earth, Rejoice

Go and enjoy choice food and sweet drinks, and send some to those who have nothing prepared. This day is sacred to our Lord. Do not grieve, for the joy of the LORD is your strength.

—NEHEMIAH 8:10

God's joy is our strength. We must remember this, especially when the battle gets fierce. The last eighteen months have been, by far, the most difficult of my life. Friends and babies have died; there has been sickness, floods, emotional trauma, huge financial needs, great loss of prosperity, life threats, slander, and betrayal. The more difficult it gets, however, the more tenacious we become to fix our eyes on the beautiful, perfect prize: Christ Jesus. He is always worth it all.

In trials and tribulations, our enemy will use every possible device to try to get us to focus on the problems. We will give him less attention and give more attention to Jesus our Savior. We will not be led astray from the simplicity and purity of devotion to Him. We are advancing. Our weapons are a firm faith, gentleness, peace, patience, and a love that cannot be resisted. In Him we cannot lose.

When we choose the low road—the only road—we never lose. When we respond in the opposite spirit—fight war with love, fight hatred with forgiveness, and repay evil with good—we always win. The Sermon on the Mount cannot be improved upon. If we follow in Jesus's footsteps to the cross—the road of mourning, meekness, mercy, humility, hunger, thirst, and peacemaking—we will truly be blessed. God, in love, turns everything around!

Why are peacemakers called sons of God on Earth? United with the Son, we continue His work of reconciliation in the power of the Spirit. The story of our struggle when we lost our base illustrates what happens when we choose our Father's perspective and walk as His very sons on Earth. God has rewarded our faith, and we have a property now in Pemba that is over seven times what we lost in 1997. Years later, the very government officials who persecuted us and beat our children have thanked us for staying in the country.

The Best Christmas Presents Ever

One day, I was facing another type of war—not from government officials, but from skeptical academics who did not believe our movement was legitimate. I was sitting on a grass mat in about 110-degree weather on Christmas Day, looking out on hundreds of our beautiful children. It was tropical African weather, and I was dripping with sweat.

I just sat there happily looking into their bright smiles because Jesus had told me, "Look each one in the eye and bless them one by one." We had invited all the children from the streets and the dump.

I listened to my Savior, and one by one, I looked them in the eye. Gathered around me were all the girls who had sold their bodies, the bandits, the rascals, the children from the village, the forgotten, the lost, the abandoned, and the lonely.

I was overjoyed to give out the presents that had been prepared by our amazing staff to the children who lived outside our center. Many of the youth had come to the Christmas party drunk. Not in the Holy Spirit—just drunk! The street girls were hardly wearing anything.

I just hugged them all. And they all called me Mama Aida.

They came one after another—hundreds of them whom we had invited to the feast. We had a co-worker from America who was a mental health director for an entire state. She thought it was rather ridiculous to try to give limited bags of toys to countless children. I think she thought I was a bit mentally ill myself.

I explained to her, "I am purposely going to give the presents first to the kids who have never gotten any presents before." So, we started giving out the presents. I was not very popular at first; all the gifts that the volunteers had spent time gathering and organizing were going to the street kids while our center kids just had to watch and wait.

But we kept handing out presents. Finally, it came down to our older girls. My friend and co-worker informed me that the bags we had left only had stuffed animals in them. Old stuffed dogs were all that remained.

So when our girls got to me, I simply asked the first one, "What would you like, sweetheart?"

"Beads," she replied.

"OK, they want beads."

My friend responded, "There is nothing in the bags but old stuffed dogs."

"Please check again," I told her. She was exasperated by this time, but she reached into the bag of old stuffed dogs and started screaming. "Beads! There are beads in the bag!" The Argentinean volunteers started jumping around, screaming for joy. All of our girls got beautiful, bright beads for Christmas.

God really is God, and He is much better than Santa Claus. I remember when I was studying for my PhD in systematic theology at Kings College, the University of London. During a seminar, one of the famous theologians teaching there smirked and commented that some pietist, charismatic types even pray for parking spots. He smugly stroked his beard and said, "God is not Santa Claus."

No, Jesus is better than Santa Claus. Jesus turned water into wine, and God is still transforming little orphan hearts into full sons and daughters of the King through His spirit of adoption.

The volunteers from that Christmas Day returned to America and Argentina to work with the poor from the inner cities. The kids who were patient enough and preferred the street children to themselves were blessed. The words St. Francis of Assisi once wrote still ring true:

> *Lord, make a channel of Thy peace that, where there is hatred, I may bring love; that where there is wrong, I may bring the spirit of forgiveness; that, where there is discord, I may bring harmony; that, where there is error, I may bring truth; that, where there is doubt, I may bring faith; that, where there is despair, I may bring hope; that, where there are shadows, I may bring light; that, where there is sadness, I may bring joy.*
>
> *Lord, grant that I may seek rather to comfort than to be comforted, to understand than to be understood; to love than to be loved; for it is by forgetting self that one finds; it is forgiving that one is forgiven; it is by dying that one awakens to eternal life.*[2]

—ST. FRANCIS OF ASSISI

Blessed are the peacemakers, for they will be called sons of God.

Devotional

Toward the end of her life, Mother Teresa reflected on her vocation and in the following quote could have been answering the questions: What? And how much depends on whom?

> The work we do is nothing more than a means of transforming our love for Christ into something concrete. I didn't have to find Jesus. Jesus found me and chose me. A strong vocation is based on being possessed by Christ. He is the Life that I want to live. He is the Light that I want to radiate. He is the Love with which I want to love. He is the Joy that I want to share. He is the Peace that I want to sow. Jesus is everything to me. Without Him, I can do nothing.[3]

Eight

BLESSED ARE THOSE
WHO ARE PERSECUTED
BECAUSE OF RIGHTEOUSNESS

*God does not demand that I be successful. God
demands that I be faithful. When facing God, results
are not important. Faithfulness is what is important.*[1]
—MOTHER TERESA

IN THE FIRST WORLD, A WORLD OF PROSPERITY AND
plenty, it seems like a paradox to be "blessed"—that is,
spiritually prosperous or joyful—when experiencing persecution. Regardless of the outward situation, even in the
midst of great suffering and pain, we must let Christ in us
be our hope of glory, our joy unspeakable (Col. 1:27).

In the first world church, there is often an escapist
mentality. We shrink away from persecution. There is no
inherent value in persecution for its own sake, but there
can be a blessing through it. When we still pray for our
persecutors to come into the saving knowledge of Jesus
and cling in the fellowship of sufferings, we can truly be
a blessed people no matter the circumstance.

Unlike the Western church, the voices of the persecuted churches in China, Africa, Asia, and South America
cry out with a different perspective. Two-thirds of the
world lives in poverty and is currently experiencing great

hardship. How can we learn to stay blessed in the midst of great pain?

Real Pain, but Beauty for Ashes

Some of us have never had a great price to pay for our faith. Others have endured extreme trials and radical tribulations. They have given their lives for the sake of the gospel.

In heaven, God promises, "He will wipe every tear from their eyes. There will be no more death or mourning or crying or pain, for the old order of things has passed away" (Rev. 21:4). Many may not know the specific pain of being persecuted for their faith. Others have been beaten, abused, raped, robbed, and have experienced their own hell on earth. To these people, God promises that He has numbered the very hairs of their head (Matt. 10:30). To our Father in heaven, all pain is real.

So how do we take our ashes and exchange them for God's beauty? How do we model God's love in the midst of abuse? How do we stay joyful even when everything is falling apart?

Jesus knew persecution like no other: "He was despised and rejected by men, a man of sorrows, and familiar with suffering....He was despised, and we esteemed him not. Surely he took up our infirmities and carried our sorrows" (Isa. 53:3–4). Jesus was misunderstood by all, even by His parents. When "He came to His own, and His own did not receive Him" (John 1:11, NKJV), how did Jesus demonstrate love to those who rejected Him again and again?

We sometimes only imagine persecution through the lens of physical suffering: being beaten, stoned, jailed, and suffering for His namesake. But there is a greater pain that comes from being rejected by those whom you love. Jesus poured forth limitless, ceaseless, bottomless love to each and every person in front of Him, regardless of the pain. Because He has known the worst pain, Jesus can relate to anything we are going through:

> Having then a great high priest, who hath passed through the heavens, Jesus the Son of God, let us hold fast our confession. For we have not a high priest that cannot be touched with the feeling of our infirmities; but one that hath been in all points tempted like as (we are, yet) without sin. Let us therefore draw near with boldness unto the throne of grace, that we may receive mercy, and may find grace to help (us) in time of need.
>
> —HEBREWS 4:14–16, ASV

Living—Not Just Dying—for Jesus

Every moment, God gives us opportunities to live for Him. What happens when we get upset and lose our patience? We lose the blessing of staying in a place of love.

Can we be joyful in the midst of any situation? Can we be happy when the government is persecuting us? How do we guard our hearts when someone close is slandering us? God gives us moment-by-moment invitations to be spiritually prosperous by staying in a place of joy—no matter what comes to rob us of our peace.

Are we only joyful when we have our own way? When we have outward circumstances to make us blessed?

We are to love those who persecute us. It is not just dying for Jesus; it is also choosing each day to live for

Him, daily dying to ourselves that others might live. It is in the little things—honoring a teacher in a class that is theologically opposed to what you believe, turning the other cheek in all situations, always choosing to prefer others no matter what—that others will see Jesus in us.

My Journey: Mexico City

The moment I met Jesus I was ruined. My life was not my own. Once you see Him, there is no turning back. I have seen His eyes. Now I can never turn away. If we die, we die for Him; if we live, we live for Him!

I started ministering on the streets at the age of sixteen, the day after I had a powerful vision. I would stand in lines at airports and wait in faith for God to provide a plane ticket. Sometimes I would be given money for airplane tickets after I left with my bags packed for the airport. Other times, I would receive money for tickets as I waited in faith in the queues or stopped at friends' houses on my way to the airport. I never told people my needs, but God always provided. In my teens, God sent me to slum areas to preach. I think my life probably breaks some rules of the missionary manuals.

God sent me to Mexico City with a team from Vanguard University of Southern California to minister to the poor. We were doing street theater among the poor when suddenly our team was grabbed by the police. They screamed and yelled at us, but God spoke to me about not reacting to my persecutors. Still, they threw us in jail.

We began to worship and thank God. Our church hosts were fasting and praying for us. We knew God was with us, but the police continued to abuse and ridicule us verbally. And then, suddenly everything changed.

One of my friends, who is six feet four inches tall, began to walk on his hands. Seeing this giant man clowning around took them off guard. They all began to laugh. Soon after, the guards, who were now amused, decided to release us.

If your reaction is meekness and kindness, then you will be blessed even if you don't feel blessed. If we had yelled or pushed back at the police, we would have lost the opportunity to choose love. We will always ask Jesus how to represent Him in each and every circumstance. In that jail cell in Mexico City, I learned to let the joy of the Lord be my strength. When we choose joy—not retribution—the kingdom of God breaks forth in the most unlikely circumstances.

Love never fails. Choosing to react in love to persecution is perhaps the godly love described in 1 Corinthians 13: "Love suffers long and is kind; love does not envy; love does not parade itself, is not puffed up; does not behave rudely, does not seek its own, is not provoked, thinks no evil; does not rejoice in iniquity, but rejoices in the truth; bears all things, believes all things, hopes all things, endures all things. Love never fails" (vv. 4–8, NKJV).

Drawn by Cords of Loving-Kindness

When you refuse to stop loving, no matter the cost, the gospel is preached beautifully. Sometimes it is not until someone watches the witness of Jesus in the midst of opposition that they receive the Lord.

My great joy is to preach in the villages and streets with alcoholics, the mentally ill, the poor, the outcasts, and the abandoned. Many of these people have great anger issues from lives full of tremendous pain.

I met a girl while preaching on the streets of London. To tell you this story, I will call her Jane. She was so angry that she basically hated everyone, especially men. She had been gang-raped by sixteen men. She had to stay in the hospital for nearly a year with complications from a broken pelvis, and she had no family or friends. She was tormented by hatred and demons, but I loved Jane.

When I met Jane on the streets, she was in her late twenties. Her hair was very short, and she was wearing men's dress shoes and a man's dark suit that was several sizes too big. It took me awhile to realize she was a woman. She had a stern, agitated appearance and was full of rage. She could not stand still even for a minute.

I also made another friend—I will call him Peter. Almost every single day for several years I would go talk to Peter and bring him food. He would yell and tell me to go away and curse at me. He did this for two and a half years. With each curse, I thought how much this man needed love, kindness, and mercy.

I kept bringing Peter potatoes and sandwiches. I refused to stop. Jesus is tenacious: He never stops loving, and He never stops giving. I just kept saying, "I love you, Peter, and Jesus loves you." Sometimes Peter would take the food; other times he would spit at me and throw it on the ground. But God's heart is relentless, and His radical love transforms the hardest of hearts.

One night Jane was so angry, she tried to beat me to death. She told me that she would slit my throat with a broken bottle that she was holding and throw me into the Thames River to die. When she tried to strangle me, all I could feel was the pain and suffering in her heart. I felt God's heart for her.

I tried to tell her, "God is in love with you. You are precious. You are called to know His love." This made her angrier!

Then Peter, who had been watching me get beaten the whole time, said he was calling the police. I told him the Lord did not want me to call them. Jane had already been thrown in jail many times, and I did not want her to suffer anymore. I wanted her to know the love of Jesus.

Peter just screamed and cursed me again.

Jane had the broken bottle, and she said she was going to rip open my face. I kept telling her again how beautiful she was and that I loved her. When I could not feel anything else, I remember praying, "God, whatever You want to do, I just want Your love to be known here."

I felt so tired; I could not take any more pain. I told Jane, "If you are going to kill me, you can just kill me. But I have to sit down."

Just as I prayed, Peter came and rescued me. He grabbed me away from Jane, started sobbing, and then he said, "For two years you told me Jesus loved me. Now I've seen His love, and I want Him. I want Him now. You kept telling me about love, but today I have seen love."

That night Peter fell to his knees and received Jesus as his Lord. We just held each other. Even in his alcoholic state, I just held him and thanked him for saving my life.

We lay our lives down for love, and we give our lives away. We cannot just love with our words. Love is in truth and in our actions.

The following week, Jane came to my house with a dozen roses for me, and she told me that she was sorry for trying to kill me. That day she asked Jesus to live in her heart too.

See Them Through the Blood of Jesus

Many people only recognize each other's faults rather than choosing to see the image of God. Hope colors the way we see each other. Grace is the lens through which we must see one another. When we see someone, we look beyond the evil of the past. We have to look through the blood of Jesus into the heart of every man—we have to peer through the eyes of the Master.

Jesus is altogether lovely, never withholding mercy, and always extending kindness: "And I will have mercy through a thousand generations on those who have love for me and keep my laws" (Deut. 5:10, BBE). He commands us to forgive seventy times seven, telling us that love always "protects, always trusts, always hopes, always perseveres" (1 Cor. 13:7). His blood is more than enough.

Recent Trial

Jesus can turn around for His glory every single opposition. Just recently, some agitators in the government were again trying to take away our Pemba property and kick us out of the country. They slandered us, spoke evil against us, and plastered lies on the front pages of the newspapers. They claimed we were contragovernment, and they broadcast this propaganda on television.

Soon after, the mayor came to visit. Even the political leaders had major doubts about us and asked the department of social justice to investigate our ministry. The public relations representative for this political party refused to remove anything from the article. They threatened to publicize even more negative reports.

All I could do was trust God. I read the Book. I had to

believe that when we were insulted or persecuted, when all kinds of evil were falsely said against us, God would win. Again we chose to sing and worship around the tent until His glory love came down.

The next day we went back to the same office that had refused to see us and had threatened us the day before. But on this day there were no guards. There were no receptionists. I brought Pastor José, one of our national leaders, with me. He prayed furiously in tongues.

I turned to him and said, "Let's go!" I told him this was our opportunity. He reminded me of how dangerous it was, but he knew God had said to go.

José kept praying in tongues. I kept telling him to be quiet as we sneaked through security locations where God had removed all the security guards. We went up the stairs and ran right into the government official in charge of propaganda.

I told this man that I refused to leave until I could speak to someone. At this point, José nearly started hyperventilating. We kept praying for the presence of God to come.

After making us wait for forty minutes, the man came back to talk with us. I told him that we were there to bless them and the government. I said, "My heart is not to hurt anyone. I am just a simple woman living and loving people for God. Maybe I do not always do it well. But I do love this country and would lay down my life for Mozambique." We talked for an hour, and I shared my heart with him.

After an hour passed, he said, "My heart was in knots because I believed you were a counterrevolutionary trying to take down my government. I will write another article.

I will speak to the president, and we will rescind our comments. This is a beautiful day."

God turned everything around for His glory. Shortly thereafter at a cultural celebration, our children danced in front of the president, with the glory of the Lord on the face of those kids who were redeemed by the precious blood of the Lamb.

On Earth as It Is in Heaven

Twice we have had the Transformations video production company come and ask to film a documentary video about the revival in Mozambique and Iris Ministries. Each time we have said no because we did not think we were transformed enough yet.

One day our communities will become so sanctified and transformed by the love of God that we will no longer need locks for our doors. Our jails will shut down. Our hospitals will be empty.

We are starting to understand that we have full access to everything for which Jesus died. Every time we go into a village that knows nothing about Jesus, we boldly ask them to bring forward all the deaf. We know that the Father promises full access to His Son's inheritance, so we step out and believe. We lay our hands on the deaf, and they hear. The children lead the way with their prayers, so the majority of the time there are many healings, and the village comes to Jesus.

If we start understanding the principles of the kingdom, we will start taking risks. We do not have to wonder if God will show up; neither do we have to beg Him to do something. Sons and daughters of God can walk with confidence, for we know that we are coheirs with Christ. And we know that we have inherited all that Jesus Himself has access to.

When we become coheirs with Christ, we learn to count suffering as joy. Jesus warned us not to be afraid to suffer. In partaking of "the fellowship of suffering with Christ," we can enter into the "power of His resurrection" (Phil. 3:10–11, NKJV). We earn the right to reign because of what Jesus already did for us.

If we are thrown in jail, we know our Father will never abandon us. If we are slandered, we know our Father will protect us. If we are stolen from, our Father will provide again. If we are stoned, we know we will feel the embrace of God around us. If we are sick, He will heal us. God is always good, all the time.

The Reward of Our Sufferings: The Harvest

Since the time we first experienced such persecution, Jesus has given us a nation to love. Since the time we first saw His face, a nation is coming to Jesus. So many laid-down laborers have responded to the call to bring in the harvest.

We have to see Him in His glory, His mercy, His beauty, and His love. We will also see Him in the poor—in the least of these. Twelve years ago we had only planted four churches, and they were very wobbly. A decade later, having experienced great persecution, we cannot count all the thousands of churches because the revival of love is spreading like wildfire across the African plains.

We really believe that you can have as much of God as you want. We cannot make revival happen, but God can. Now we cannot go back, no matter what the cost, no matter what the persecution. We understand what

Paul meant when He wrote, "I consider that our present sufferings are not worth comparing with the glory that will be revealed in us" (Rom. 8:18).

Recipe for Revival

> Then He said to His disciples, "The harvest truly is plentiful, but the laborers are few. Therefore pray the Lord of the harvest to send out laborers into His harvest."
>
> —MATTHEW 9:37–38, NKJV

The Beatitudes are God's recipe for revival. When we become one with our Bridegroom King, we become Jesus in the flesh to a lost and dying world. He is our model. He is perfect theology. If we imitate Jesus, people will see Him when they look at us.

God was on a mission when He sent His Son from heaven to Earth to save you. Now that the harvest is ripe, God is calling forth a new breed of sent-out ones, a generation of laid-down lovers who will run into the darkest corners of the earth, call in the outcasts, bring in His bride, and compel the poor to come to the wedding feast.

We believe God is calling a generation forward to be laid-down lovers for Him, to walk in the ways He walked, and to follow His Sermon on the Mount as their instructions for their Christian walk.

You do not have to look far to see Jesus in the eyes of the dying, the broken, and the lost. He came with ceaseless love for both the one and also the masses. Now we must do the same: stop for the one, but believe for multitudes. This is the face of revival.

We are called to carry His glory, but first we must

lie down to ourselves so that whole nations can come to Jesus. When we learn to lie down, no matter the mourning, the suffering, or the persecution, we will inherit heaven on Earth.

The Beatitudes are our recipe for revival. They are a portrait and description of Jesus. When we walk as Jesus walked, we will be blessed.

Blessed are those who are persecuted because of righteousness, for theirs is the kingdom of heaven.

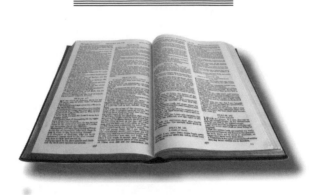

Devotional

I am the vessel. The draft is God's. And God is the thirsty one.[2]

—Dag Hammarskjold

I know you through and through—I know everything about you. The very hairs of your head I have numbered. Nothing in your life is unimportant to Me. I have followed you through the years, and I have always loved you—even in your wanderings.

I know every one of your problems. I know your need and your worries. And yes, I know all your sins. But I tell you again that I love you—not for what you have or haven't done—I love you for you, for the beauty and dignity My Father gave you by creating you in His own image.

It is a dignity you have often forgotten, a beauty you have tarnished by sin. But I love you as you are, and I have shed My blood to win you back. If you only ask

Me with faith, my grace will touch all that needs changing in your life. I will give you the strength to free yourself from sin and all its destructive power.

I know what is in your heart—I know your loneliness and all your hurts—the rejections, the judgments, the humiliations. I carried it all before you. And I carried it all for you, so you might share My strength and victory. I know especially your need for love—how you are thirsting to be loved and cherished. But how often have you thirsted in vain, seeking that love selfishly, striving to fill the emptiness inside you with passing pleasures—and ending with even more pain. Do you thirst for love? "Come to Me all you who thirst" (John 7:37). I will satisfy you and fill you. Do you thirst to be cherished? I cherish you more than you can imagine to the point of dying on a cross for you.

I thirst for you. Yes, that is the only way to even begin to describe my love for you: I thirst for you. I thirst to love and to be loved by you—that is how precious you are to Me. I thirst for you. Come to Me, and I will fill your heart and heal your wounds.

If you feel unimportant in the eyes of the world, that matters not at all. For Me, there is no one any more important in the entire world than you. I thirst for you. Open to Me, come to Me, thirst for Me, give Me your life—and I will prove to you how important you are to My heart.

No matter how far you may wander, no matter how often you forget Me, no matter how many crosses you may bear in this life, there is one thing I want you to remember always, one thing that will never change: I thirst for you—just as you are. You don't need to change to believe in My love, for it will be your belief in My love that will change you. You forget Me, and yet I am seeking you every moment of the day—standing at the door of your heart, and knocking.

Do you find this hard to believe? Then look at the cross; look at My heart that was pierced for you. Have you not understood My cross? Then listen again to the words I spoke there—for they tell you clearly why I endured all this for you: "I thirst" (John 19:28). Yes, I thirst for you—as the rest of the Psalm verse, which I was praying says of Me: "I looked for love, and I found none" (Psalm 69:20).

All your life I have been looking for your love—I have never stopped seeking to love and be loved by you. You have tried many other things in your search for happiness; why not try opening your heart to Me, right now, more than you ever have before.

Whenever you do open the door of your heart, whenever you come close enough, you will hear Me say to you again and again, not in mere human words but in spirit: "No matter what you have done, I love you for your own sake." Come to Me with your misery and your sins, with your troubles and needs, and with all your longing to be loved. I stand at the door of your heart and knock…Open to Me for I thirst for you.[3]

—MOTHER TERESA

Epilogue

Your attitude should be the same as that of Christ Jesus: Who, being in very nature God, did not consider equality with God something to be grasped, but made himself nothing, taking the very nature of a servant, being made in human likeness. And being found in appearance as a man, he humbled himself and became obedient to death—even death on a cross! Therefore God exalted him to the highest place and gave him the name that is above every name, that at the name of Jesus every knee should bow, in heaven and on earth and under the earth, and every tongue confess that Jesus Christ is Lord, to the glory of God the Father.
—PHILIPPIANS 2:5–11

MANY YEARS AGO, JESUS CAME TO ME IN A VISION. A bright white light surrounded me, and I heard an external, audible voice from God for the first time in my life. I was sixteen years old.

Jesus told me that I was to be married to Him. Oil ran down my arm, and I felt Him kiss my left ring finger. He said, "You are called to be a minister and a missionary. You are called to Africa, Asia, and England." When the heavy, weighty presence of God lifted, I was alone in the church. I had been motionless with my hands raised for nearly three hours.

There God called me to give my life for the poor. There Jesus called me to a life of intimacy with Him.

Incredible joy hit me, and the next day I began to speak on the streets of the Indian reservation where I lived as an America Field Service student. I have been speaking for Him and living a life of a sent-out one ever since.

Jesus was the ultimate sent-out One. God Himself was on a mission when He sent His Son from heaven to Earth to save us. He emptied Himself of heaven's riches—all for love's sake. He is our model.

Prisoners of Love

Like Jesus, we have only one aim and goal: to love. Our mission is passion and compassion; we are to love God and to love our neighbor.

All that Jesus did flowed from that abandoned place of laid-down love. With *compassion* He embraced the man with leprosy, held the dying woman, broke the law to sit at the well, and talked to the prostitute:

> But when He saw the multitudes, He was moved with compassion for them, because they were weary and scattered, like sheep having no shepherd. Then He said to His disciples, "The harvest truly is plentiful, but the laborers are few. Therefore, pray the Lord of the harvest to send out laborers into His harvest."
>
> —MATTHEW 9:36–38, NKJV

Ministry is being one of these sent-out ones—a laborer of love. If ministry is not about compassion and passion, let it die.

Jesus is the ultimate example of God dwelling among us. Love Himself walked the earth. We fix our gaze on Jesus as the perfect model of life. After studying the Beatitudes, we must ask: What did Jesus do before preaching His famous Sermon on the Mount?

The answer is, before He preached on the kingdom, Jesus demonstrated it. He healed diseases and helped those suffering from severe pain and demon possession. He preached the gospel.

Learn to Love

We believe when we die and go to heaven, God will expect the same from us that He did from His Son. He will ask us only one question: Did you learn to love?

I am greatly moved by the words of Mother Teresa, who perfectly expresses this sentiment with us:

> Love has no meaning if it isn't shared. Love has to be put into action. You have to love without expectation, do something for love itself, not for what you may receive.[1]

> Love in action is what gives us grace. We have been created for greater things...to love and to be loved. Love is love—to love a person without any conditions, without any expectations. Small things, done in great love, bring joy and peace. To love, it is necessary to give. To give, it is necessary to be free from selfishness.[2]

We are created to bring the love of Jesus to those who are in need. Love looks like something, yet it has no limits.

God did not say the poor will always be good, kind, or thankful, and yet He always calls us to love them.

The Simplicity of the Gospel

God has called us to this simplicity of love. I do not feel called to what many call greatness or success. This is why I love the Beatitudes so much, as they are my life message. My only call is to love more. The Beatitudes teach us that true love may cost everything. It may cause pain, but at the same moment, it may bring joy.

I ask Jesus for more courage to love without limits. God has called His bride to be carriers of His glory. To do this, we must deepen our life of sacrifice, prayer, and abandoned love. To be true, love must empty itself of "self."

Ministry is all about love. In Philippians 2, Paul—who was, after Jesus, one of the greatest sent-out ones to walk the planet—writes: "If you have any encouragement from being united with Christ, if any comfort from his love, if any fellowship with the Spirit, if any tenderness and compassion, then make my joy complete by being like-minded, having the same love, being one in spirit and purpose..." (vv. 1–2). Paul exhorts us to have the same kind of heart, motivation, and love as Christ Jesus. Love is tender. Love is filled with compassion. This exhortation lived out would change the very face of Christianity.

Learning to Love

Love will cost you everything: laying down your life, living a life of passion and compassion, giving without expecting, feeling God's very heartbeat, surrendering to

His rhythm, and following the Lamb wherever He goes—even to the ends of the earth.

Why go to the ends of the earth if you have nothing to give? The only currency that will heal every culture is ceaseless love. To be a minister, we must walk like Jesus, talk like Jesus, and be like Jesus for a broken and dying world.

Ministry looks like servanthood manifested through love. Your job description is to be the fragrance of Christ, the beauty of Jesus, and the very anointing of Him on Earth. As you minister, you minister in Him. As you walk, you walk in Him. Jesus told the Father:

> I pray also for those who will believe in me through their message, that all of them may be one, Father, just as you are in me and I am in you. May they also be in us so that the world may believe that you have sent me. I have given them the glory that you gave me, that they may be one as we are one: I in them and you in me. May they be brought to complete unity to let the world know that you sent me and have loved them even as you have loved me. Father, I want those you have given me to be with me where I am, and to see my glory, the glory you have given me because you loved me before the creation of the world.
>
> —JOHN 17:20–24

Go Deeper: Union and Communion

Union and communion: this is the essence of Christianity. We must give up all that we are in order to possess all that He is. We must yield who we are to become one with

Him. The first part of your calling is intimacy with Him. If you are not in love with Jesus, I loudly cry, "Quit!" until you find His love so that you can carry it to others.

Don't go out to share Him unless you are in love with Him. When you are in love with Jesus, then all you do will radiate Him.

It is to the degree that you are in love that you radiate Him. If you are not in love enough, then you need more time with Him. My life is busy. But the busier I get, the more time I need with Jesus. When I minister, I must minister out of the fullness of my unity with Him. Our first pleasure is to be united with Jesus—to be one with the man Christ Jesus.

First Commandment in First Place

Our greatest joy in life is to be married to Jesus so that we can give our lives away without fear, just as He did for us. My goal, even in this book, is that you fall so deeply in love with Him that there is not a *no* left in you when responding to the high calling of God in Christ Jesus. When you are full of the presence of God and another person meets you, it is the same as that person meeting Him. Jesus becomes irresistible to them. When you hold them, Jesus holds them.

Missions and ministry are simply about laid-down passion at the foot of the cross, praying, "Possess me, Holy Spirit, that I might be conformed into the image of Jesus. Let me reflect the majesty of who He is." Let Jesus love you first so that you can love others as He did. When you lose yourself inside His huge heart, you find only pure joy in Him.

Love God, and Love Your Neighbor

Our mission statement for Iris Ministries since 1980 is simple: love God; love our neighbor. This is our plan. We will love God with all our heart, mind, soul, and spirit, and love our neighbors as ourselves. We will be one with each other and one with Christ Jesus—for this Jesus died.

What is God's goal? That every single person in this world would know Him. That every man, woman, and child would be taken in as His sons and daughters. That His house would be full.

He made heaven big enough for everyone. His desire is for the beauty of His kingdom to be manifest on Earth. Because Jesus died, there is always enough. How can the gospel go forth to the ends of the earth so that none should be left an orphan? The apostle Paul answered this very question by writing:

> If then there is any comfort in Christ, any help given by love, any uniting of hearts in the Spirit, any loving mercies and pity, make my joy complete by being of the same mind, having the same love, being in harmony and of one mind; doing nothing through envy or through pride, but with low thoughts of self let everyone take others to be better than himself; not looking everyone to his private good, but keeping in mind the things of others. Let this mind be in you which was in Christ Jesus.
>
> —PHILIPPIANS 2:1–5, BBE

This is the reason we give up our homes, our countries, and our possessions. It is not so we will look like we are doing something good. We give everything to

God as we follow the Lamb who was slain. We choose another lover. We choose to be married to Him. If we choose that, then in Him we have all that we need; there is more than enough.

New Ministers: The Laid-Down Lovers

Ministry is not about where you are or where you go; it is about where He is. His love knows no limits or boundaries.

A new breed of ministers is rising up who will not wear out for the gospel. They are so caught up in passion, unity, and fullness that they run out and say, "World, here I come!" If they go into places where they get shot at, they are thrilled. If they do not get shot at, they are thrilled. If the place they go is filthy, they are thrilled. If it is clean, they are thrilled. Jesus is the joy set before them. He is their exceedingly great reward.

God has to move on the inside of us. We have to feel His heart before we ever have anything to offer anyone else. Then, when we have rested our heads against His chest, like John the Beloved, we can move and go out to others according to His heartbeat.

Despite traveling hundreds of thousands of kilometers last year, I find myself at home everywhere I go. When I am in Korea, I love Korea. When I am in Brazil, I love Brazil. When I am in the United States, I love America. And when I am on the university campuses, I love the universities. Of course, Mozambique is truly home to me and is my favorite place on the earth.

When I know that God has sent me, I am happy wherever I am. I live for Him. It is all about this passion; it is all about where He is. All I care about is union with Him and embracing the one in front of me.

Righteousness, Peace, and Joy in the Holy Spirit

Ministers should be the most joyful, in-love people on the planet. It is not a competition in misery. Like Paul writes in Philippians 3:4, 7, "I myself have reasons for such confidence. If anyone else thinks he has reasons to put confidence in the flesh, I have more.... But whatever was to my profit I now consider loss for the sake of Christ."

I have been shot at five times, beaten, thrown in jail, slandered, and had many death threats on my life, so I know a tiny little bit about suffering and pain. But that is not the part of my life that brings God the most joy.

Of course, we are very ready to endure any and all suffering when necessary. The point, however, is not the suffering itself. The point is obedience and whole-hearted abandonment to God, whatever the circumstances look like.

Like Paul, we have learned to count it all joy. If you want to export misery, then find another profession! Joy is contagious. If we are not full of Him, we have nothing to offer anyone else. We must become unstoppable in love. Of course, there have been times when I felt pain and discouragement, when I have been sad or tired. Many times I just wanted to go and live in a cave as a "monkess" because Jesus is always wonderful and people are not always nice. Yet, as I focus on the grace and goodness of God, the joy eventually returns.

Unstoppable in Love

The Beatitudes show us how, through any kind of suffering, like Jesus, we will ultimately be blessed. Ministry ought to be the most contagious, outrageous Holy Spirit adventure on this side of heaven.

While in the hospital in October 2005, I almost died of MRSA (methicillin-resistant *Staphylococcus aureus*). I said, "I will not die of a flesh-eating disease. I want to be a martyr for Jesus."

It is easy to die for Jesus, but it is more difficult to live fully for Him. I do not want to just die well; I want to live well for Him. Until my last breath, I want to give everything that I am for all that He is. As Mother Teresa wrote, "You love until there is pain; you love through the pain, until all that remains is love." If you are really in love, then it is a joy to suffer for the gospel.

If you are feeling pain, get deeper and closer to His heart. Press in for His face-to-face presence. Nothing will seem difficult when He is only a breath away. You too will be compelled by love. I know the Beatitudes are all true. God is worthy to be praised through any crisis, and in the end we will be blessed.

The amount of crises that I deal with in any given day is ridiculous. If I were not in love, I would be in a mental institution. But I am not in a mental home because I am in love. When crises come to me and press in on me, one after another, I just have to look into the eyes of the One I love. He is always enough!

A Cup of Suffering and Joy

In the year 2007, the Beatitudes were my lifeline as I learned more than I ever imagined about the cup of suffering and joy. Our nation of Mozambique was hammered with floods, cyclones, and monster waves; Pemba, Cabo Delgado, was hit with cholera; and a few kilometers from our Zimpeto children's center in Maputo, a large munitions dump blew up, spraying mines, missiles, and scrap metal for thirty kilometers. Hundreds of people were killed. Houses were leveled, leaving victims crushed beneath the rubble.

We had never seen such suffering before. But true to this passage, we had rarely seen such blessedness in our lives. As I stood in the ruins of a house leveled by a missile and held a weeping woman in my arms, I drank of His cup of suffering. As I embraced Marcelina, Edwardo, and Carvalho, who were orphaned by the blasts, I drank His cup of suffering.

After driving all day through the mud and potholes of Zambezia to minister and deliver food to a distant village devastated by floods, I rocked a tiny starving baby in my arms and tried to no avail to find milk. I drank the cup of His suffering.

After arriving in Caia, a region torn apart by cyclones, I spoke to the director of a large nongovernmental organization. He was evacuating his workers and helicopters after the cyclones because he could not get past all the corruption and red tape. I drank of the cup of suffering, knowing that those helicopters could have saved the lives of the many precious people stranded in the flood.

But in this suffering, we are blessed beyond measure. I also drank His cup of joy. God opened the door for us to provide food to fourteen refugee camps in the Zambezia province. I drank the cup of joy while watching my Mozambican spiritual son Norberto and my Brazilian spiritual son Herbert lead the relief effort for the province. I drank the cup of joy while seeing the faces of hopeless, desperate people run to meet King Jesus. They gave their lives to Him and thanked Him for saving their lives.

Worship to our beautiful Savior reached heaven in Zimpeto when the children, co-workers, and missionaries gave glory to God for sparing their lives as missiles and mines flew in every direction above them and around them. I listened to the testimonies of children who were rescued from the streets, thanking Jesus for holding them in His arms as the terror of the blasts continued all around them.

Pastor José spoke of the amazing opportunity God had given all of them to worship in the middle of the frightening chaos. Missionaries shared how they would gladly give up their lives to protect the children, and I drank the cup of joy.

We offered a home in our center to the homeless children, and I watched their tears turn to laughter.

Our Dwelling Place

For *Christ's love compels us*, because we are convinced that one died for all, and therefore all died. And he died for all, that those who live should no longer live for themselves but for him who died for them and was raised again.

—2 CORINTHIANS 5:14–15,
emphasis added

When we are compelled by love, when we embrace the life of the Beatitudes, we are truly blessed. Truly we are filled with inexpressible joy knowing we dwell in the shelter of the Most High God. We rest in the shadow of the Almighty. He is our refuge and our fortress; we put our trust in Him. He covers us with His wings of love, and we find safety in Him.

We must choose to follow the Sermon on the Mount and act in a way that releases the kingdom of God in each situation. We must choose to be peacemakers, to fight back only with more love and more forgiveness, and to believe God is always good and knows how to father His children.

When the kingdom of God manifests on Earth, it creates a new order of righteousness and peace. Trouble has come to our nation, and we have opened our eyes and seen the pain. We have opened our ears to hear the cry of the desperate, and so we drink His cup of suffering.

We have opened our hearts to Him, and He is our dwelling place. He loves us. He rescues us and commands His angels to surround us. We have called on Jesus. We have acknowledged Him.

But we also drink His cup of joy, knowing that because He died there will always be enough. There is enough for nations; there is enough for an entire world. Every drop of His blood cries out to us, "I love you. I heal you."

We are blessed beyond measure. We are transformed by His love; therefore, we transform the world around us. When we are truly compelled by love, then ours is the kingdom forever and ever. Amen.

Notes

One: Blessed Are the Poor in Spirit

1. Mother Teresa, *In My Own Words*, comp. José Luis González-Balado (New York: Gramercy Books, a division of Random House Value Publishing, Inc., 1996).

2. Ibid.

3. Mother Teresa, *No Greater Love*, ed. Becky Benenate and Joseph Durepos, rev. ed. (Novato, CA: New World Library, 1997). Originally published as *The Mother Teresa Reader: A Life for God*, comp. LaVonne Neff, rev. ed. (Ann Arbor, MI: Servant Publications, Inc., 1995).

4. Ibid.

5. BrainyQuote.com, "Jim Elliot Quotes," http://www.brainyquote.com/quotes/quotes/j/jimelliot189244.html (accessed March 24, 2008).

6. Mother Teresa, *In My Own Words*.

Two: Blessed Are Those Who Mourn

1. Malcolm Muggeridge, *Something Beautiful for God: Mother Teresa of Calcutta* (New York: Harper & Row, 1971, 1986).

2. Mother Teresa, *In My Own Words*.

Three: Blessed Are the Meek

1. Mother Teresa, *No Greater Love*, 3.

2. T. T. Mundakel, *Blessed Mother Teresa: Her Journey to Your Heart*, English trans. ed. (Liguori, MO: Liguori Publications, 2003).

3. Ibid.

Four: Blessed Are Those Who Hunger and Thirst for Righteousness

1. Mother Teresa, *No Greater Love*.

2. Ibid.

Five: Blessed Are the Merciful

1. Mother Teresa, *In My Own Words*.

2. Mother Teresa, *No Greater Love*, 164.

Six: Blessed Are the Pure in Heart

1. Mother Teresa, *In My Own Words*.
2. Muggeridge, *Something Beautiful for God*.
3. Mother Teresa, *In My Own Words*.
4. Mother Teresa, *No Greater Love*, 3.
5. WorldPrayers.org, "Mother Teresa—In Her Own Words," http://www.worldprayers.org/frameit.cgi?/archive/prayers/meditations/prayer_is_not_asking.html (accessed May 15, 2008).
6. Mother Teresa, *A Gift for God–Prayers and Meditations* (New York: Harper and Row, 1975).

Seven: Blessed Are the Peacemakers

1. Mother Teresa, *Like a Drop in the Ocean*, trans. William Hartnett (New York: New City Press, 2006), 1. Originally published as *Wie ein Tropfen im Ozean*, ed. Wolfgang Bader (Munich: Vertag Neue Stadt, 1997).
2. Irwin Abrams and Tore Frangsmyr, eds., *Nobel Lectures: Peace 1971–1980* (Singapore: World Scientific Publishing Co., 1997), 229.
3. Mother Teresa, *My Life for the Poor*, eds. José Luis González-Balado and Janet N. Playfoot (New York: Ballentine Books, 1987).

Eight: Blessed Are Those Who Are Persecuted Because of Righteousness

1. Mother Teresa, *In My Own Words*.
2. BrainyQuote.com, "Dag Hammarskjold Quotes," http://www.brainyquote.com/quotes/authors/d/dag_hammarskjold.html (accessed March 27, 2008).
3. Margaret Hebblethwaite, ed., "Wednesday of Holy Week," *The Living Spirit: Prayers and Readings for the Christian Year, A Table Anthology* (Lanham, MD: Sheed & Ward, a division of Rowman & Littlefield Publishing Group, 2000), 169.

Epilogue

1. Mother Teresa, *One Heart Full of Love* (Ann Arbor, MI: Servant Publications, 1988), 87.
2. Mother Teresa, *No Greater Love*.